P9-DTQ-732

DISCARD

NEW ROADS
TO
DEVELOPMENT

NEW ROADS TO DEVELOPMENT

Raanan Weitz
Foreword by M. J. Rossant

A TWENTIETH CENTURY FUND ESSAY

Contributions in Economics and Economic History
Number 64

Greenwood Press
New York • Westport, Connecticut • London

Library of Congress Cataloging-in-Publication Data

Weitz, Raanan, 1913-
New roads to development.

(Contributions in economics and economic history,
ISSN 0084-9235 ; no. 64)
"A Twentieth Century Fund essay."
Bibliography: p.
Includes index.
1. Economic development. 2. Economic policy.
I. Title. II. Series.
HD75.W45   1986   338.9   85-21979
ISBN 0-313-25177-0 (lib. bdg. : alk. paper)

Library of Congress Catalog Card Number: 85-21979
ISBN: 0-313-25177-0
ISSN: 0084-9235

First published in 1986

Greenwood Press, Inc.
88 Post Road West
Westport, Connecticut 06881

Printed in the United States of America

The paper used in this book complies with the
Permanent Paper Standard issued by the National
Information Standards Organization (Z39.48-1984).

10   9   8   7   6   5   4   3   2   1

To Rivka, our children, and grandchildren,
the font of continuity

CONTENTS

LIST OF TABLES

FOREWORD

The international debt crisis has brought a halt to development in the so-called Third World, and with it development planning. Indeed, for some time now, a number of authorities have been claiming that development planning is dead. But that is not the view of Raanan Weitz, a longtime apostle of development planning. To the contrary, he approached the Twentieth Century Fund a few years ago with the thesis that it was time for development planning to take a new step forward, striding toward an integrated approach to development planning that did not rely on the intellectual tools derived from the experiences of already developed countries, which all too often result in serious imbalances in developing economies, with productive manpower going unused, and urban areas suffering from overconcentrations of people and problems.

In a sense, Weitz was in agreement with critics of development planning. For it has long been his view that planning could not continue to go on as it always had. In *From Peasant to Farmer*, his first work for the Fund, he set out the rudiments of an integrated approach based on the family farm in a rural community. In his new book, which is drawn from his lifelong experience in development and his work with colleagues at the Rehovot Settlement Study Centre in Israel, he has evolved a theory of development that calls for coordinated planning to maximize the growth of the agricultural, industrial, and service sectors. It is his belief that social planning is critical to constructive development, but social planning that involves the people being planned for every step of the way. He argues against planning from above, whether put in place by authoritarian bureaucracies or by a corps of outside planners who, no matter how well meaning, have no knowledge of those who are being planned for.

Raanan Weitz is first and foremost a humanist, and if planners will listen with an open mind to what he has to say about people and their needs and desires, and then apply that knowledge to a development plan, they will be taking a step in the right direction. If politicians can abandon grandiose plans for big projects, and instead provide the least developed areas of their nation with the means of slow, steady growth at a basic level, they will be creating the possibility for a better life. What Raanan Weitz has done is point out the path to effective development. We hope that planners will heed his advice.

M. J. Rossant, Director
The Twentieth Century Fund
October 1985

ACKNOWLEDGMENTS

I wish to express my deepest appreciation and gratitude to all those who contributed toward the research, writing, and publication of this book.

First and foremost, my thanks go to the Twentieth Century Fund for making it all possible: to the director of the Fund, Mr. Murray Rossant, for his assistance and guidance throughout, and particularly for the faith and support he gave me during the long struggle with the difficult and tortuous subject of the book; to the program officers of the Fund, Mr. Gary W. Nickerson and Mr. Steve Andors, for their objective and constructive criticism; and last but not least, my sincere appreciation goes to Ms. Beverly Goldberg who molded the book into its present shape with great understanding and care.

My deepest gratitude to the research team at the Settlement Study Centre in Rehovot who persevered through all the trials and tribulations in the long period of analysis and discussion.

Foremost among my collaborators stands Dr. Jacques Silber for his most valuable contributions, especially on the subject of the optimal mix and the various econometric calculations linked with it. Appendix B was written entirely by him, and he should be given full credit for it.

The team included:

- Mrs. Levia Applebaum, for her merciless, though nicely edged criticism and analysis.

- Prof. Alexander Berler for his penetrating and broad views of the human and social problems.

xvi   Acknowledgments

- Miss Ruth Perlman for her contribution in the chapters dealing with mobility and spatial planning.
- Mr. Avshalom Rokach for his meticulous gathering and analysis of data throughout the final set-up of the study questionnaire, and the lengthy research which followed.
- Dr. Roberto Soldinger for his extensive literature survey.
- Mr. Yosef Gotlieb for his substantial research and editorial assistance.

Thanks are also due to the following for their contributions:

- Dr. Daniel Freeman for the collection of material at the World Bank Headquarters in Washington and for further data and analysis on the state of developing countries.
- Dr. Nezer Menuhin for his contribution on the subject of government structure and organization in developed and developing countries.
- Dr. Naomi Nevo for her remarks and contribution on the subject of social patterns.

In choosing the ten countries as suitable samples for the research project, we were greatly assisted (in 1978) by advice generously extended by scholars of world renown, namely: Thomas Balogh (Oxford University), Brian J. L. Berry (Harvard University), Simon Kuznets (Harvard University), Walter M. Rostow (University of Texas), Paul P. Streeten (World Bank), and Albert Waterston (World Bank).

Special thanks are due to all those institutions and persons who helped us by filling out our most unusual and complicated questionnaires, by digging into past histories, and hunting for present data off the main and conventional stream of surveys. They include:

- The Marga Institute—Sri Lanka Centre for Development Studies, and Mr. D. Rajendra, former secretary of Local Government and Home Affairs in the Ministry of Public Administration.
- The Korea Research Institute for Human Settlements in Seoul, and Mr. Choi Chung Bok, a senior researcher at the Institute.
- The Centre for Urban and Regional Studies (Centro Urbanos y Regionales) in Buenos Aires, Argentina; Dr. Jorge D. Hardoy from this Centre, as well as Mr. Beatriz Aguirra Martin, a research trainee at the Centre.

- Dr. Isaac Aviv and Mrs. Aviva Aviv from St. Antony's College in Oxford, who were kind enough to complete the questionnaire for Spain, and who travelled to Spain for that purpose.
- The Bartlett School of Architecture and Planning at the University College, London; Dr. Michael Safier, Research Director of the Development Planning Unit at the college, as well as Prof. Walter Elkan and Dr. Nici Nelson.
- The Faculty of Social Science at the Hitosubashi University in Tokyo, Japan, and Prof. Nasatoshi Yorimitsu of that faculty.
- The Institute of Social Studies at the Hague, Netherlands; Prof. J. G. M. Hilhorst from the Institute, as well as Mrs. Jacques Robert.
- The Expert Group on Regional Studies, Ministry of Industry, Stockholm, Sweden; Dr. Costa Goteland of the Expert Group, and Mr. Bernt Jacobson.

Thanks are also due to the Economic and Social Data Division of the World Bank, Washington, D.C., for providing us with World Tables tapes, where much of the relevant data was stored.

Last, but not least, I owe my gratitude to Mrs. Leah Aharonov for her initial editing of the manuscript; Ms. Debora Hesse, who polished the English language prior to editing and who typed the manuscript; and Mrs. Erna Philip who typed several tiresome and confused drafts.

To all of the above and to some whose names I have inadvertently missed, I owe my thanks for making it possible for me to write and complete this book.

Raanan Weitz
Jerusalem
February 1985

PREFACE

My work at the Rehovot Settlement Study Centre in Rehovot, Israel, is development planning. I have spent long years trying to bring about economic growth in both Israel and other developing nations, often serving as a consultant to the United Nations and several other international and national authorities. My experience has taught me the value of firsthand experience, of getting to know the people for whom you are producing plans, and of learning how the society for which you are planning works down to the smallest and seemingly most inconsequential detail. I have seen development plans work, and I have seen them fail. I have seen the effects of national politics on planning, and I have seen the effects of international problems—both economic and political—on planning. The best made plans are affected by so many—and so often unexpected—events that development planning can be a frustrating endeavor. Analyzing what went wrong and what went right with a plan sometimes means trying to take into account once-in-a-lifetime events, and because of the lack of previous data gathering and record keeping, it sometimes means working with incomplete data and data that cannot be easily compared with other data.

When I discussed the need for action with my colleagues at the Study Centre, we came to the conclusion that a lack of adequate—and perfectly comparable—data was not enough to preclude an examination of the type presented in this book. Working together at that stage meant that the analysis was based on much more than data, it was enriched by cumulative years of experience and a belief that something not only must be done but can be done. Today, when the plight of the developing nations is the stuff of headlines—particularly their debts, which are shaking the international economy, and the famines that are wreaking havoc in Africa—I believe this more than ever. Such catastrophic events are the result of basic problems that will not be solved without a new approach to both planning and implementation. Indeed, planning initiated for political reasons, or for credit, and worst of all, planning in emulation of the West, has been responsible for some of the problems.

That kind of planning must be replaced. The time has passed for building factories in cities unprepared for their advent, factories that create slums and misery in the cities and destroy traditional life in the villages from which their workers are drawn. And the time has passed for building elaborate dams that take years of effort and seemingly endless funding but, when finished, the water is not utilized.

This book is the product of an extended research project undertaken by an interdisciplinary team of specialists at the Centre, experts in economics, geography, sociology, organizational behavior, management, and development planning. We began by gathering and analyzing a vast amount of data through a thorough survey of the existing literature and then by requesting international organizations dealing with Third World development to formulate their reactions and attitudes for an all-encompassing approach to development. But our own main effort was concentrated on trying to penetrate in depth into the workings of development changes by preparing a specially designed questionnaire for the countries chosen as a representative sample. The data provided us with new understanding of several important phenomena both in time and space.

We would have preferred a far broader data base, but we think the nations we examined provided the information needed to lay the groundwork for future development planning.

Once this was done, we shared our experiences and brought in others to discuss theirs. Then we looked at the problems facing the people of the developing nations and decided on the steps that might be taken to help. Those first steps arc what this book presents. I hope that it will provide the impetus to development planning of a new kind, planning grounded in the lives of the people being planned for, in their national life, and in the world in which they live.

NEW ROADS
TO
DEVELOPMENT

_____ CHAPTER 1 _____

THE DEVELOPMENT STRUGGLE

While humanity shares one planet, it is a planet on which there are two worlds, the world of the rich and the world of the poor. The world of the rich is industrialized, technologically advanced, and relatively affluent; the world of the poor is economically under-developed and marked by extreme poverty, with a great majority of its people leading wretched lives from birth until untimely death. This polarization of humanity, which is a fairly recent phenomenon, is an outgrowth of the use of technology that took place during the past two centuries.

Technology has wrought profound socioeconomic structural change, raising the already high standards of living attained in the most industrialized countries. For example, Leontief[1] has estimated that the mean income in Austria is expected to rise to $9,300 by 1990, a sharp increase from the mean income of $5,900 recorded in 1976.* By the year 2020, per capita income in Austria should be $22,000, a predicted fourfold increase in average income within two generations.

Not only have mean incomes in the industrialized countries increased dramatically, but the economic gaps between classes in many of these nations have also consistently decreased. In Sweden, for example, the difference between the highest 10 percent and lowest 10 percent income groups was 11:1 in the 1950s; by 1980, the difference had shrunk to 5:1. Current tendencies, extrapolated for the lowest plausible rate of economic growth, suggest that the gap between the two extremes of the Swedish income scale should be no

*These figures are in constant dollar, 1976 prices.

more than 2:1 by the year 2010. Of course, the Swedes enjoy enviable prosperity and have distributed their wealth to conform with egalitarian principles espoused by social democrats, but the same economic trends can be seen in many other industrialized nations.

The computer, the single most powerful tool since the rise of industrialized agriculture, has already begun to transform the way that people in the richer nations work, study, or spend their leisure time, creating a Second Industrial Revolution. In these nations, mechanization, the hallmark of the First Industrial Revolution, is now well on its way to being replaced by automation.

Automation has affected all economic sectors in these nations. In agriculture, the farmer is able to create an artificial environment in which computers allow the optimum use of soil, water, and environmental conditions. And with artificial environments, genetic engineering, and automated drip irrigation, new conditions for agricultural production are being predicted; for example, some suggest that grain yields will soon more than double current yields. The savings anticipated from industrial automation are tremendous. Industrial robots and digitally controlled automated machines can already design, analyze, tool, manufacture, inspect, and store products on the basis of computer graphics and simulations. And computerization has already begun to change dramatically the service sector.

THE PROMISE OF THE FUTURE IMPERILED

Unfortunately, the great promise of affluence and material well-being may never be fulfilled. The reason is simple: as one part of humanity readies itself for unprecedented prosperity, the developing nations, home of the vast majority of the world's population, are tottering on the brink of an apocalypse.

The poverty of the developing countries has become endemic and is already a way of life for most of the inhabitants of this planet. According to the International Bank for Reconstruction and Development (the World Bank), 800 million people live today under conditions of "absolute poverty."

More than three quarters of a billion people have barely enough income to keep themselves alive from week to week. In the low-income countries people on an average live 24 years less than they did [*sic*] in the industrialized countries. Some 600 million adults in developing countries are illiterate; a third of the primary school-age children (and nearly half of the girls) are not going to school.[2]

To be sure, the World Bank acknowledges that important gains have been made in the Third World over the past thirty years. Average income has tripled, life expectancy rose from 43 to 54 years, and the proportion of adults who are literate rose from approximately 30 percent to more than 50 percent of the total during this period. This progress notwithstanding, poverty continues to fester throughout the developing countries. As described by the World Bank report:

As much as four-fifths of their income is consumed as food. The result is a monotonous, limited diet of cereals, yams or cassava—with few vegetables and in some places little fish or meat. Many of them are malnourished to the point where their ability to work hard is reduced, the physical and mental development of their children is impaired, and their resistance to infections is low. They are often sick—with tropical diseases, measles, diarrhea, and cuts and scratches that will not heal. Complications of childbirth are a common cause of death. Of every 10 children born to poor parents, two die within a year, another dies before the age of five; only five survive to the age of 40. The poor have other things in common, apart from their extremely low incomes. A disproportionate number of them—perhaps two in five—are children under the age of 10, mainly in large families. More than three quarters of them live in (often very remote) rural areas, the rest in urban slums—but almost all in very crowded conditions. . . .[3]

The statistics are still more distressing when it is realized that, even if the relative rate of population growth were to be stabilized, which is unlikely, the absolute number of people living in poverty would continue to rise.

In addition to the absolute poor, hundreds of millions of other people live in varying degrees of squalor and privation throughout the developing world. The number of people living in the thirty-four poorest countries was about 2,000 million in 1981; the average per capita gross national product (GNP) for these people was approximately $270 per year. In contrast, the sixty countries comprising the middle-income group of nations had a population of 1,128 million at that time. Average per capita GNP in these countries of $1,500 per year appears to be a veritable fortune compared with the corresponding figures for the poorest countries.

However, when the status of the middle-income nations is compared with that of the 719 million people living in the nineteen most industrialized countries (excluding the nations with centrally planned economies in East Europe), their situation is seen for what it really is: just a cut above abysmal poverty. The per capita GNP of the developed industrialized countries is seven times that of the middle-income nations and *forty* times that of the poorest countries.[4] The per capita GNP, however, is an inadequate indicator of economic standing, since it does not describe the distribution of resources within a soceity.

The recognition of a wide and probably unbridgeable chasm between the rich and poor nations became general after World War II. Before that time, it was believed that the difference in economic productivity between the rich and the poor nations would be transitory; the devastation visited on European economies as a result of the conflict had obscured the structural differences between the two worlds. The Marshall Plan, the World Bank, and other programs created to help the European countries recover sought to "provide the monetary and financial machinery that would enable nations to work together, thus aiding political stability and fostering peace among nations."[5] The purpose of the World Bank was described in terms of reactivating the European engine of the world economy through capitalization. It was presumed that the "trickle-down effect" would enable Third World countries to benefit from Europe's recovery.

By 1944 when the World Bank was created at the Bretton Woods Conference, the belief that improvement would accrue to the poorest nations was already fading. For example, John Maynard Keynes, the neoclassical economist, stated at the conference that:

It is likely in my judgment that the field of reconstruction will mainly occupy the proposed Bank in its early days. But as soon as possible, and with increasing emphasis as time goes on, there is a second primary duty lain upon it, namely to develop resources and productive capacity of the world, with special reference to the less developed countries.[6]

The idea that the poorest nations were suffering from economic crises that were—at least in effect if not in origin—comparable to the havoc wreaked in Europe was spreading, but that the differences were structural was not readily understood. The poorest nations were thought merely to have tarried along the route to development taken by the richer nations; the developing countries were considered "underdeveloped" relative to the industrial nations.

Only during the 1960s did the entrenched nature of poverty in the developing world become apparent. Some observers argued that the magnitude of capital and technology transferred had not been sufficient to generate the levels of growth needed. But other planners and economists had begun to sense that capital alone could not lead to development. The United Nations, prevailed upon by its Third World majority of member-states, issued a proposal that sought to

reduce disparities and remove inequities. It is to help the poorer countries to move forward, in their own way, into the industrial and technological age so that the world will not become more and more starkly divided between the haves and have-nots, the privileged and the less privileged.[7]

The embryonic UN strategy for development was based on the premise that industrialization had to be the priority for those nations. The premise was embraced by both the Western industrialized nations and the Eastern bloc nations. Since the capitalist nations were industrialized, they were perceived to be developed. Hence it was assumed that industrialization alone would lead to development. The Soviet bloc had also banked its development on industry rather than agriculture; their economic failures in this respect had not yet been recognized. Therefore, both the Common Market countries and the COMECON nations counseled industrialization as the road to development.

The industrial program was adopted by the United Nations in the proclamation declaring the 1960s as the Decade of Development. The goal sought was a minimum of a 5 percent yearly rise in per capita income within the developing nations by 1970, and this was to be achieved by the concurrent transfer of technological know-how, equipment, and investment capital from the richer to the poorer nations.[8]

The rate of economic growth targeted for the UN's First Development Decade failed to materialize, as the level of foreign aid did not even remotely approach the magnitude sought. The policy-makers charged with development found themselves utterly unable to control the situation. As a result, the World Bank convened an investigatory commission, the Pearson committee, to investigate the predicament. The committee concluded that industrialization could not generate the employment opportunities needed by the ever-increasing populations of the poorer nations. The programs of the Development Decade had not, they found, anticipated the limits imposed by population pressures on arable land, and they determined that the current agrotechnology was incapable of meeting the food needs of the masses in the developing world. The committee also stressed that disparities in income levels within the developing countries had expanded the gap between rich and poor in these societies. These conclusions were also being reached independently by many development specialists.

In view of the new assessment of the situation, the 1970s was designated the "Second Development Decade" by the United Nations. The broadly defined goal was to "improve the quality of life in order to create better and healthier communities."[9] To accomplish this, community development on the local level, as opposed to concentrating efforts on the national level, was instituted, and agriculture, rather than industry, was emphasized. Development projects were to "increase the agricultural productivity and enhance the standard of living in the developing world."[10]

Despite the mobilization of resources, wholesale socioeconomic change did not come about. Many nations, once known for their self-sufficiency, could no longer feed their own populations. The number of families living below the poverty line was—and still is—mounting. Symptomatic of the overwhelming difficulties in the developing world was the growth of social unrest and violent revolutionary activity.

The situation had deteriorated so drastically and in such a short period that another international commission of inquiry, under the chairmanship of former West German chancellor and social democratic leader Willy Brandt, was launched. The Brandt commission released its findings in a report entitled *North/South: A Program for Survival.*[11] The report, heralded before its release as a document of the utmost importance, was later dismissed as "misleading" and "one-sided" by many scholars and planners. The reactions to the Brandt report's dire forecasts of problems that could threaten the very survival of civilization were more a protest against the remedies it prescribed than an attack on the validity of its appraisals. Essentially, the Brandt report proposed a two-pronged strategy to counteract the impending crisis. It called for

a substantial increase in the transfer of resources to developing countries in order to finance:

(1) Projects and programs to alleviate poverty and to expand food production, especially in the least developed countries.

(2) Exploration and development of energy and mineral resources.

(3) Stabilization of the prices and earnings of commodity exports and expanded domestic processing of commodites.[12]

The report also strongly stressed the critical importance of income distribution and emphasized the perils ensuing from expanding income gaps between the elite and nonelite classes in the developing nations. The report recommended extensive intervention by Third World governments to bring about greater equity in the allocation of economic wealth within societies. The commission advocated that Third World governmental involvement assume elements of both neoclassical market reform and principles of centralized planning.

The remedies put forth incurred the ire of critics. Kenneth Minogue, for example, commented on the report in *Between Rhetoric and Fantasy*, describing it as engaging in:

administrative fantasies about "massive transfers of wealth," and . . . melodramatic talk about global crisis of a kind now so familiar to us that it has become rather like the little boy who kept crying "Wolf!"[13]

P. D. Henderson also argues that the Brandt report advocates unrealistic remedies:

It is clear that the rich countries at present feel unable to adopt broad measures of economic expansion, and that if they wished to do this the means are already at their disposal. They could perfectly well increase the buying power of their own people (for example, through lower taxes), and the reasons which deter them from acting in this way applies equally to the idea of higher transfers to foreigners.[14]

In other words: since the developed countries have exhibited no inclination to reallocate wealth within their own nations, it is unrealistic to expect them to transfer wealth abroad.

Despite its shortcomings, the Brandt report offers the best description of the development challenge presently available. Although the commission presented few solutions, it has contributed mightily to the search for answers by succinctly posing the right questions. Up to now, development efforts have been based on programs that did not derive from empirically grounded, comprehensive analytic frameworks. Development projects have generally been ad hoc responses to vexatious problems. However, the scope and complexity of poverty faced in these nations are so formidable that they dispel conventional notions concerning the very nature of the development process. Significant progress in the struggle to eliminate poverty cannot be made until the essence of development is completely understood.

TOWARD A DEFINITION OF DEVELOPMENT

A survey of the literature reveals that there is little consensus among experts concerning the basic elements and processes involved in development. An enormous amount of professional material has been written, of course, and various concepts and remedies have been put forward. The kinds of solution suggested are, for the most part, outgrowths of disparate academic disciplines. The economist, sociologist, geographer, and experts in other disciplines involved in development think and act in terms of their own particular fields, and, consequently, many aspects of development are treated without reference to societal realities. This situation not only makes for disjointed, segmented, and unsound planning and implementation of development schemes, but it renders the very meaning of the term "development" unclear and elusive.

Many scholars in the field equate development—explicitly or implicitly—with economic growth. Accordingly, an overwhelming majority of the plans designed for developing countries deal with economic growth alone. This is confirmed by Gunnar Myrdal in *Asian Drama*:

In the writing on development problems of underdeveloped countries, it is commonplace to acknowledge that a close relationship exists between the effectiveness of development policies in the economic field and prevailing attitudes and institutions. But it is fair to say that almost all studies of these problems, whether by South Asian or foreign economists, imply an almost complete neglect of this relationship and its consequences. In particular, all the development plans suffer structurally from this defect. Prejudice derived from Western "Marxist" thinking—which on this as on so many other points converge—and given support by vested interests or inhibitions in policy formation, blur economists' broader insights into South Asian conditions and confine their range of vision to "economic factors."[15]

In the recent rush to "put out the fire" in the Third World, the term "economic growth" has been understood as referring to two main issues: (1) the production capacity of a nation vis-a-vis its ability to meet primary material needs and (2) the distribution of the fruits among different sectors in the society.

Most of the professional literature dealing with development refers only to these processes and the economic factors that affect them. However, a review of the accumulated data stemming from planning schemes in the developing countries indicates that economic factors are not sufficient to explain the workings, successes, and failures of development projects.

The often contradictory definitions of development that are arbitrarily used by specialists reflect the confusion surrounding the essential nature of the development process. For example, Everett M. Rogers writes that:

Development is a type of social change in which new ideas are introduced into a special system in order to produce higher per capita incomes and levels of living through more modern production methods and improved social organization.[16]

While Michael P. Todaro contends that:

Development . . . is concerned with the economic and political processes necessary for affecting rapid structural and institutional transformations of entire societies in a manner that will more efficiently bring the fruits of economic progress to the broadest segments of their populations.[17]

Norman Jacobs offers a third definition:

Development is used to denote the maximalization of the potential of a society, regardless of any limits currently set by the goals or fundamental structure of the society.[18]

Despite their divergence, the above definitions share the implicit premise that development and economic growth are identical; attempts to distinguish between development and economic growth are the exceptions rather than the rule.

As a result, specialists are trying to identify other factors not previously taken into account that appear to influence the effect of projects in the field. Such factors are usually classified as "social," "institutional," or, in even more general terms, "noneconomic" conditions. There is a general consensus among specialists today that economic factors are integral to the development process. But the significance of "noneconomic" factors in the process, and the nature of such factors, are the subject of a great deal of continuing debate. For example, Everett E. Hagen observes that:

Almost every economic analyst studying economic developments agrees that some non-economic factors are of importance. However, when an economist presented his analysis he often ignored other factors, because he claimed no competence with respect to them. And of course, ignoring them when making prescriptions is equivalent to assigning them zero importance.[19]

This characterizes the work of many economists dealing with economic growth—Balogh, Kaldor, Leibenstein, Rostow, Lewis, Nurske, Eckaus, Hirschman, and Mason—who stress the importance of noneconomic factors in development but who rarely take them into account when making concrete proposals. Even those definitions that do not assume that development is exclusively economic growth fail to explain development. For instance, George Dalton writes: "Development is growth plus change and the change involves the society as a whole."[20]

The confusion that surrounds the definition of the term "development" reflects the absence of a comprehensive analysis concerning all of the elements that make up development. Unless and until there is a clear understanding of the development process in its entirety, all activities aimed at ameliorating the plight of the world's poorest nations are essentially doomed to failure. Therefore, a reexamination of the basic factors shaping society, and a thorough consideration of the relationship between the individual and society, must be central to an effective effort aimed at socioeconomic change.

A DIFFERENT DEVELOPMENT PROGRAM

The ultimate goal of this work is to describe a different pragmatic and effective strategy for the developing nations that fuses the four aspects—economic, spatial (the distribution of population and production across a nation), institutional, and social—involved in development into an integrated program.

As pointed out by Albert Waterson, "Although some good statistical and other data may be found in almost every country, planning in most less developed countries is severely handicapped by widespread lack of information."[21] The first step in preparing this book was, therefore, to assemble an adequate data bank. A special questionnaire was prepared to acquire both general information and more specific statistics dealing with the national, regional, and local levels of economic functioning. Particular emphasis was placed on the latter two levels, since that is where the most glaring statistical gaps exist. In order to identify trends characteristic of growth in the past, and to understand how it could be promoted in the future, information was sought for the years 1870-80, 1920, 1950, and 1970-75.

Once the questionnaires had been prepared, a relatively small number of countries were selected for intensive scrutiny. These nations were chosen because they represent various stages of development and various types of earlier involvement with developed nations that have had an effect on their subsequent growth and development, and because, given the realities of development, they are nations in which probing for necessary data would be successful. The nine nations chosen for this intensive examination and their per capita GNPs are: Sri Lanka ($200), South Korea ($820), Argentina ($1,730), Israel ($2,850), Spain ($3,190), the United Kingdom ($4,420), Japan ($5,670), the Netherlands ($7,150), and Sweden ($9,520).*

The objective in preparing and analyzing the questionnaires was to uncover patterns governing changes in attitudes, behavior, production structures, and consumption trends inherent to the process of economic growth at different stages in the evolution of societies. After locating public institutions familiar with the historical and contemporary conditions of their respective nations that were willing and able to participate in the inquiry, each cooperating country was visited, sometimes repeatedly.** Once the questionnaires were completed, various empirical analyses of the information were carried out.

An analysis of the development literature revealed a lack of inquiry into the historical processes that shaped and continue to mold developed and developing countries. Conventionally, the development challenge has been cast in terms of the present, as though some lofty methodological principle would be served by isolating current development issues from those of the past; in attempting to identify the components of development, there has been woefully little effort made to understand their coevolution. In addition, the search for understanding of the development process has been side-tracked by attempts to determine indicators for economic growth that overcome the deficiencies intrinsic to the per capita GNP index. The formulation of such additional and alternate indicators is sorely needed; nevertheless, measurements alone will not provide an adequate definition of development and will not lead us to a comprehensive development strategy.

I believe that understanding development requires understanding "values." A major reason for the recurrent failures of past development efforts is the neglect to involve values systems in development planning and implementation. Development, in the

*All the calculations for the questionnaire and the tables in the book, unless otherwise noted, are based on constant dollars of the year 1977.

**The patterns uncovered were described not only for the national level, namely averages for the entire population of each country for each stage, but also for the local level and the regional level. It will be clear later that this unique, simultaneous description for the three levels is very significant.

Dev not same as economic growth

most general sense, is the process of change in human society that occurs simultaneously among individuals and in society as a whole. In terms of this study, the definition must add that the changes should bring about a sense of satisfaction to the average individual of the society.

The fulfillment of the economic needs of the individual depends on the ability of the system of production to provide for those needs, and to ensure equitable distribution among all the members of the society. Development differs from economic growth in that it must recognize and deal with the fulfillment also of other needs and aspirations of individuals. These needs are *not* the outcome of the production system; nor are they connected—directly or indirectly—with the production system. These needs and aspirations are considered "values." *Development, in brief, is economic growth concurrent with modifications in the systems of values.*

THE PLACE OF "VALUES" IN DEVELOPMENT

For this definition to be effective and useful, it is necessary to clarify the term "values." Values—as opposed to instincts—are needs that originate in the intellectual capacity of men. "Men are not indifferent to the world, they do not stop with a merely factual view of their experience."[22] Since man has become aware of the world surrounding him, he has developed more than an instinctive reaction to those surroundings; he also has intellectual attitudes that are later translated into emotional reactions and expressed in daily attitudes. Although human behavior is motivated both by instinct and intellectual reasoning, it is important to distinguish between the origins of our reactions.

Unfortunately, the term "value" is used very widely and assumes different meanings, each reflecting once again the disciplinary education of the user. In the professional literature, the term as used by economists assumed a more philosophical meaning.[23] In the literature dealing with development problems there is quite a distinct and increasingly noticeable trend of associating values with development.[24]

The debate over the relationship between values and development, or, better, between values and economic growth, is steadily growing.* Opinions range from one extreme to another—from those who maintain that the key to understanding today's problems in the developing world is to be found chiefly, if not exclusively, in the nebulous realm of the undefined value system, to those who shrug it off with the very simple and straightforward declaration that "Differences about policy among disinterested citizens derive predominantly from different predictions about the economic consequences of taking action . . . rather than from fundamental differences in basic values."[27]

For the purposes of this book, a theory of values is considered essential. The theory starts from an understanding that in any society an individual, in order to achieve well-being, needs many things—values—that have nothing to do with economic growth and that development plans aimed at economic growth will not succeed if the values of the society are destroyed in the process of trying to achieve economic growth. The list of values is a long one, varying from universal values to those that change from community to community and from society to society.

BASIC AND SOCIAL VALUES

Basic values are those values that determine relations between the individual and the society in which he lives. Therefore, they apply to all individuals of a particular society. "Faith," for example, is a basic value: the need for it is not affected by the permutations of the system, and it is universal. It can be broadly defined as belief in transcendent existential meaning or universal wisdom. It can be, but is not necessarily, expressed by a religious creed.

Man has the ability to understand his own mortality. The knowledge of death—not feelings about it—provides the sources of

---

*Probably the first contribution in the field of economics to the definition of value came from Adam Smith, who said that the word "has two different meanings and sometimes expresses the utility of some particular object, and sometimes the power of purchasing other goods which the possession of that object conveys. The one may be called 'value in use'; the other, 'value in exchange.'"[25] A. Marshall rejected this interpretation and preferred to define value as the expression of the relation between two things at a particular place and time.[26] The argument over definitions of value continued for a while, then slowly the discussion about the term "value" in an economic context receded into history.

various phenomena unique to mankind: for example, suicide and capital punishment (as punishment, per se, not actions resulting from the necessity of obtaining food, a mate, territory for survival, etc.).

Endowed with this knowledge, the human being cannot reconcile himself to it. Even though this attribute remains with man constantly and accounts for the very essence of his being, he cannot exist or function without a network of "antibodies" to protect him from the knowledge and from the feeling that his existence is not more than a fleeting adventure, void of any particular significance. Because it is universal, this value is independent of the values of society, which, as we shall show, are variable and dependent on the economic system. The weight of these "antibodies" changes in accordance with technological innovation (which motivates economic growth) and with alterations in man's conception of the world (resulting from developments in the natural sciences), but the "antibodies" are present and provide a reason for living. This is intricately entwined with faith, namely, belonging to something that is both transcendent and meaningful.

The system of basic values, according then to this view, has, at its heart, both the sense of continuity and the sense of belonging. Continuity makes the individual an inseparable link in the chain of generations, rooted in the past and continuing into the future, and provides an emotional link that makes it possible to view life as more than a transitory episode.

The source of the feeling of continuity stems from the framework of the family in its broadest sense, that is, the emotional aspects of the family and not necessarily the family as a social, economic, or organizational institution. The family has undergone profound modifications as a result of economic growth; nevertheless, it remains the source of continuity.

The other major element of the system of basic values is the individual's sense of belonging to the world around him. When the individual's sense of belonging emanates from the depth of his internal emotional structure, he enjoys the tranquility that stems from the explicit understanding of his mission in life.

The ancient Hebrews expressed it thus:

Keep in view three things and thou wilt not come into the power of sin.
Know whence thou comest and whither thou goest and before whom thou

art to give strict account. Whence thou comest,—from a fetid drop. Whither thou goest,—to the place of dust, worms and maggots and before whom thou art to give strict account,—before the King of Kings, the Holy One blessed be He.[28]

These few lines succinctly describe the predicament faced by mortal man. The knowledge of having to "account" to someone in the end is actually a consolation that each of us is not just an unimportant speck but a significant element in a world ruled by a "universal widsom"—the wisdom of God.

The belief in the divine is directly related to the knowledge of the existence of a "universal wisdom" that rules the entire universe and all of its phenomena, and it is this belief that led to the growth of the individual's feeling of belonging to the world surrounding him—the world of man and the universe of God. The basic values shield man from the eternal dilemma of comprehending the purpose of his life.

The basic values, which are expressed in distinctive ways by different societies, nonetheless invariably contain core elements that provide the individual with a feeling of belonging and a feeling of continuity. The first lends meaning to temporal existence: the individual belongs to a community to which he or she is integral. The community is most often defined by familial and/or geographic parameters, but they may include national, linguistic, or even ideological or academic communities as well. The feeling of continuity overcomes belief that life is but a transitory and insignificant episode of accidental origins.

By contrast with basic values, social values are those values that determine relations between the individual and the society in which he lives. Social values can be theocentric and ancient in their origins (as in many traditional societies), or they may be atheistic and derived from recent sources (as in the case of the so-called Communist states). Hence they apply only to individuals of a particular society.

Whether tacitly or explicitly, social values are interwoven into a *social pact* that governs the interaction between a society and the individuals that comprise it. Sometimes the social pact assumes the form of written constitutions, state ideologies, or national creeds. In other cases, social pacts are unwritten but nonetheless present and authoritative. They may exist on the village, tribal, national, or international level. They constitute boundaries of social life that spell out society's and the individual's rights and responsibilities to each other.

Social pacts are symbolized by a variety of instruments, ranging from national anthems, flags, public ceremonies, and other expressions of patriotism or civic pride. Social pacts go under a variety of names and labels and have been widely studied by political and other social scientists. Development specialists, though, have not recognized the importance of social pacts and do not know how to apply or change them for the purpose of facilitating socioeconomic change. And yet social pacts are fundamentally important to the development process.

THE IMPORTANCE OF VALUES SYSTEMS TO DEVELOPMENT

A great deal of erosion in values systems has taken place in Western societies, particularly with respect to basic values. This erosion has led to pervasive alienation of the individual in the rich industrialized countries—as exemplified by suicide rates, alcohol and drug abuse, criminal activity, and other trends destructive to both the individual and society. Against this backdrop, it is clear that, while the industrialized nations have demonstrated impressive rates and levels of economic growth, they have neglected to give the necessary attention to upholding values. As a result, while the nonindustrialized nations are exceedingly poor, most are not now afflicted with the same kind of spiritual poverty that marks many industrialized nations. While the priority of the developing countries—indeed, of the entire world if cataclysm is to be avoided—must be to eradicate the prevalent material poverty, the road to economic growth should not be strewn with the ruins of previously useful values systems.

The values aspect of development has been ignored mainly because of the inability of specialists to include them in quantitative models. A narrow interpretation of scientific method is to assume that if a phenomenon cannot be measured its significance is marginal. So far as societal development is concerned, this view must be discarded: values, though not quantifiable, must be treated as if they were as important a component of development as economic growth if development planning is to succeed.

A DEVELOPMENT FRAME OF REFERENCE

Development is the process of change that occurs in human society, consisting of economic growth and changes in the systems of values.

Economic growth must be understood as having two dimensions, the temporal (representing the expansion of the production system, wealth, and efficiency) and the spatial (corresponding to regional distributional aspects). Both dimensions will be useful only if certain persistent misconceptions concerning the way that economic growth can be fostered are relinquished.

The per capita GNP index reflects only changes in national wealth and production capacity over time, but economic growth also takes place at varying rates and intensities at different levels of society. For example, the introduction of a tractor on an individual farm is hardly felt on the national level, though it has tremendous and immediate impact for the family working that farm. Similarly, spectacular increases of mineral output in a country may not be readily apparent to the peasant working land in the same region. Growth is therefore expressed in one way on the local level and in a completely different way on the national level.

But the picture of development is not complete without the noneconomic factors. These include values systems and other social and organizational elements that determine the internal dynamics of the society. The changes that take place in this sphere are qualitative and not quantitative ones, but despite their intangibility, they fulfill a central role in development.

Development is the progressive change in the society's status quo that takes place as a result of new and dynamic relationships between different socioeconomic forces. Development dynamism, the product of change involving all infrastructures—economic, spatial, institutional, and social—of society, is a strange—and nonlinear—phenomenon that can restructure a nation's socioeconomic base.

Development dynamism explains why a given nation can experience economic growth relative to another nation without being more developed than the poorer nation: the way in which the fruits of economic growth are distributed is certainly as important as increases in national wealth and production capacity. In my terms, and those are the terms that inform this work, the economic betterment of elites, even Third World elites, does not reflect development if the masses of nonelite citizens sink further into the morass of poverty. Instead, more modest increases in the economic system, along with the progressive improvement of the socioeconomic structures, produce development.

Development consists of the simultaneous change in all spheres of activity—in the temporal and spatial dimensions of economic growth, in the values system, and in the societal dynamism. The development specialist must seek to create conditions that provoke the necessary concurrent changes in all activities through a focused and systematic coordination of economic, sociological, geographical, technological, medical, educational, and other development factors. While there may be short-run priorities in terms of which area needs to be dealt with first, each area is equally important in the long run.

Society must be seen by the development specialist as a dynamic, organic entity, not as a static one. The introduction of changes in the technological base of society affects every other aspect of the society.

THE PROPELLANT FORCES OF GROWTH

Public and private forces are the twin dynamos of the development process. These forces have been extensively described in the economic literature of the past century and a half. Capitalism favors private forces in its economic system. (There are, of course, differences of opinion among those who declare themselves proponents of capitalism: some classicalists repudiate government intervention in the economy, some support government intervention when it is necessary to render the market free of unfair competition or to correct market failures, and some favor more extreme government intervention.) On the other hand, socialists basically favor a centrally planned and directed economy—directed by state, party, trade union, syndicate, or other collective entities. (Here too there are differences of opinion, ranging from belief in a mixed economy to belief in a communistic society.) Classical Marxists, syndicalist Maoists, and other orthodox socialists agree that the national economy should not be the domain of private interest groups.

Supporters of both capitalisms and socialisms agree that there is an inherent tension within the economic system between individual interests and public ones. The supporters of capitalism seek to eliminate or at least curtail the limits imposed by society on private initiative, while those in favor of socialism aim to prevent the exploitation of society by the individual.

From the development point of view, both orthodox capitalism and dogmatic Marxism have proven to be unrealistic. They both distinguish between, and belligerently champion, opposing sides of the public versus private polarity. However, contrary to both orthodox theories, these forces are not mutually antagonistic. They can complement each other, with each force predominating at different stages of economic growth. By applying these forces in specific combinations, the tension between them can be harnessed to benefit development progress—a general rule for the optimal combinations of these forces that can be applied to maximize economic growth in various development situations exists. This book will thoroughly discuss—and present the rationale for—what I consider the optimal combination of these distinct forces for various stages of economic growth. These combinations, or *optimal mixes*, change because structural transformations occur in the socioeconomic base of a society as it advances through the development process.

The schedule of optimal mixes can be used as policy guidelines for successful development activity. The development of a society can be directed according to my Development Frame of Reference. Such a theoretical framework, defined in later chapters, is posited on the belief that structural change is the product of a shifting relationship between economic, spatial, institutional, and social structures. The purpose of the development frame of reference is to systematize a planner's awareness of the relationship existing between different levels of society at various stages of development.

DEVELOPMENT IN A NEW LIGHT

Development activities to date have been largely aimed at emulating the way development took place in the industrialized nations, forgetting that the realities of today are substantially different. These activities have also mistaken cultural similarities for growth. A nation where English is spoken impeccably and afternoon tea is ritualized is not necessarily a nation that is developed. On the other hand, a nation where a unique linguistic, cultural, and religious tradition thrives along with an economy that meets the primary material needs of the masses *is* a developed society. The other mistake is to assume that where there is economic affluence the basic needs of the people have been maintained. In this sense, real development has not been achieved in the industrialized nations.

The approach to development described below does not pretend to be free from subjective judgments. My belief in egalitarianism, popular participation in the development decisionmaking process, and cultural pluralism in dealing with the values systems of different peoples underlies this approach.

The approach to development advocated here is based on the thesis that the development of the poorer nations of the world will come about only by the travail of the developing peoples themselves. For structural reasons spelled out below, foreign aid, though desirable as a catalyst for development, cannot in and of itself develop a poor nation. The transfer of capital and technology can, if appropriately and carefully channeled, expedite the development process. But the magnitude of capital required for this task is gargantuan, and it is unrealistic to press such claims for funds. Development must occur as a result of socioeconomic change originating in the developing society itself.

In order to counteract the human misery of those in developing countries, intense and protracted intervention, of a kind without precedent in history, is necessary. But it should be informed by a consciousness of the myriad aspects involved in the development process. The integrated approach to development is the only one, I believe, that stands a chance of succeeding.

During a professional lifetime, first as a farmer, then planner, and finally policymaker in a developing society, as well as experiences in numerous developing countries, I have seen the development challenge from the grass-roots perspective of peasants and workers as well as from the bird's eye view of government. The inevitable conclusion of this life-time's experience is that the two perspectives must be merged, since they both reflect the same reality.

In order to effect sound development, the specialist must know where the society has been and where it should go. Development must carry with it an understanding of the society's past and a vision of its future. The term "development" is a relative one. It defines societal change *from* one status *to* another. Therefore, an understanding of the past, present, and future of developing societies must be a prerequisite to development planning.

CHAPTER 2

DEVELOPMENT PRIORITIES

What is life like for the poor in a poor nation?

In Baluchistan, a province in eastern Iran, Ahmed Fazbollah, a peasant, works the plot of land he inherited from his father, who inherited it from his father, and so forth for generations. During these long years, the life of the Fazbollah family has changed little: they still draw water from the same well their forefathers did, they till the same soil, and they do it all with the same rudimentary tools.

The *quanat*, a network of underground infiltration tunnels that brings water to the farm from an aquifer at the foot of the mountains fifty kilometers away, is the lifeblood of the Fazbollah's farm and those adjoining it. According to ancient lore, the *quanat* system was constructed by the Emperor Cyrus, who reigned over the land 3,000 years ago. The system, which has survived invasions, wars, earthquakes, and other calamities, waters the semi-desert soil, thus enabling Fazbollah and his neighbors to eke out a living. The water is allocated among the farms according to a schedule developed long ago. Since rainfall is infrequent and of little value in this district, life would be impossible without the *quanat*. And so the Fazbollahs look upon the *quanat* as a gift of life from the gods of old, whom they still honor in accordance with folk traditions that predate the family's conversion to Islam centuries ago.

On his five-hectare plot watered by the *quanat*, Ahmed Fazbollah cultivates mostly wheat, the staple of the area. He also plants barley in the winter and sorghum in the summer to provide food for his draft animals—a pair of mules that are considered a sign of relative wealth to his neighbors, who own only donkeys. He also devotes a small area to growing legumes, chickpeas, and beans, and around his house, he has planted a few fruit trees and vegetables. In addition, he is raising some chickens and a small number of sheep, which are slaughtered for use at the traditional festivals, the highlights of community life.

Fazbollah does not attempt to grow anything for market, for there is no market within reach. The farm always provided just enough food for the family and the payment of taxes, usually between one-tenth and one-fifth of what the farm produced. Then, about a generation ago, things began to change. Ahmed, like those of earlier generations, was raised to think of his family as his greatest treasure: three generations living under one roof—the farm couple, the two or three children of the ten or twelve born to them who manage to survive childbirth and the diseases of infancy, and their parents, who are too old to work. Within this family setting, traditions flourished and life was basically tranquil. Occasionally, war took its toll, and natural disaster struck, but these were accepted as part of life, a life that was hard and always very poor but ultimately peaceful and satisfying.

By the time I got to know Ahmed Fazbollah, his life had been changed. Some of the changes were the result of development plans aimed at improving life for the peasants; for example, an infirmary had been built in the main village of the district. In time, because of improved access to health care, more children survived infancy and the old began to live longer. Of course, this was a blessing, but then, as the nonproductive members of the population began to increase, the food supply proved inadequate. The youths of the village, realizing that something had to be done to prevent starvation, began leaving the village for the towns and cities in search of a livelihood.

Some went to Tehran and other major cities, but many young men from other areas had had the same idea, and after a while, some returned, hungry, disillusioned—and angry—for they had seen the palatial homes of the rich, those who controlled the incredible wealth that came from the petroleum exported to the industrialized world. These bitter young men cannot reconcile the glitter and extravagance of the life of the rich with the life their families endure. They question the meaning of their existence—and the validity of their beliefs. They debate, at times violently, their place in and their relationship to a society that is beset by social, economic, and political turmoil.

The challenge to development planners is to prevent the complete erosion of the way of life treasured by Ahmed Fazbollah—and the campesino in the Peruvian Andes, the *fellah* in Egypt, the peasant in China—and yet to provide the material means needed to support that life. The development specialist should try to plan in such a way that living standards steadily improve; that is, the economy must grow enough to withstand the effects of such positive improvements as an eradication of hunger, disease, high rates of infant mortality, illiteracy, and inadequate housing. The result, of course, involves a transformation of society, but it should be a transformation in keeping with the traditions that made that society a good one for its people.

TRADITIONAL EQUILIBRIUM: A DESCRIPTION OF A LOST WAY OF LIFE

The changes that Ahmed Fazbollah described to me mark the destruction of a way of life that endured for centuries. Within much of the developing world today, the ways of Fazbollah—traditional subsistence agriculture—are still typical of life for most people. The social relations between rural communities in poor nations and in the urbanized sectors within their countries and the rest of the world were, until fairly recently, quite limited. Insulated from the outside world by geographical and technological constraints, rural communities in the poor nations—and until the First Industrial Revolution, those in what are today the indus-trialized nations—were entirely self-sufficient. The economic foundations of these societies, based on traditional subsistence agriculture, as T. Schultz notes, often represented the most efficient exploitation of the resources available to them—so long as the population remained within certain limits.[1]

The social and cultural structure surrounding the subsistence basis of traditional economies were remarkable for their stability. Although reliable historical records are few, there is strong anthropological evidence indicating that socioeconomic stability, such as that enjoyed by the Fazbollah family for thousands of years, was typical of traditional life.[2] Although the superstructures in such societies changed, often dramatically with respect to the regimes ruling a country at a given time, such changes had little effect on the economic, physical, institutional, and social structures within the society. The culture and language of a new ruler might influence the native people, causing changes, but they were changes that rarely affected the crops grown, the manner in which they were cultivated, the system of irrigation employed, or the way tools were fashioned. The way in which the typical *fellah* in the Middle East functioned in his workaday world, for example, remained remarkably constant through changing regimes from the seventh century (and probably even earlier) through Persian, Arabian, and Turkish domination until European colonialism in the nineteenth century.

The stratification of traditional society was dictated by the very nature of subsistence agriculture. It took eight to nine farming families to sustain one nonfarming family, such as those involved in the priesthood, aristocracy, or warrior-nobility. In other words, such a traditional society could sustain no more than 10 to 15 percent of the population as a nonfarming elite class. Accordingly, the status of the peasant farmer applied to the great majority of citizens in the society, which ensured stability and constancy in the socioeconomic structures of the society. For these reasons, I call this period from the beginning of sedentary agriculture to the First Industrial Revolution, Traditional Equilibrium.

MODERN EQUILIBRIUM

The mechanization and reorganization of production, especially in terms of scale, that were the essence of the First Industrial Revolution rapidly eroded Traditional Equilibrium in the nations in which the revolution took place. Urban areas grew in size and number, "pulling" workers from the countryside to the nascent industrial centers, which were situated for reasons of economy in already urbanized areas. Mechanical technologies were pressed into service within the agricultural sector, in order to make it possible for farmers to support more than the traditional 10 to 15 percent of the population as nonfarmers. The rise of capitalism, both a cause and effect of the First Industrial Revolution, brought the expansion of surpluses to unparalleled levels. Capital, the medium through which surpluses were exchanged, was reinvested in the economy, bringing even greater productivity to the evolving economic system.

In the West, the technological innovations of the First Industrial Revolution radically altered society. Geographical mobility of individuals within a society, a function in part of the need to attract labor from rural areas to industrialized urban ones, served to undermine extended families and other kinship patterns. Increasingly, secularism and the spirit of the European enlightenment took hold and reduced the influence of traditional creeds and kinship patterns. Ownership of land was transferred from feudal aristocrats to landowners who converted the estates from subsistence agriculture to market-oriented cash crops. The latter development was part of a process that produced the market economy.

This economy, though present as a marginal aspect of economic life during Traditional Equilibrium, expanded radically and became the dominant form of economic relations after the First Industrial Revolution. Crops were no longer solely a staple for the physical sustenance of the farm family, but became a commodity to be sold and traded on the market for capital. In order to support the market economy, roadways and other physical infrastructures were created. As a result, a third economic sector, the service sector, began to expand. New relations of production came about: the majority of workers sold their labor in exchange for wages that were then used to acquire essential goods and services from the market economy. In its more advanced stages, where the enlargement of the market became imperative, capitalism spawned imperialism, whereby new markets and sources of raw material and labor were obtained in what has become known as the Third World.

Traditional Equilibrium had lasted for hundreds, and in some cases thousands, of years. The First Industrial Revolution transformed the economic basis of society in a fraction of that time. As stated by Robert Heilbroner some twenty years ago:

Nothing is more remarkable, when we compare the happenings of our time with those of a generation ago, than the extraordinary change in the scale of world events. . . . During the middle years of the twentieth century we have actually been spectators at an unprecedented enlargement of human affairs, an enlargement which may well appear in the future as one of the great watersheds in human history.[3]

Since those words were written, even greater change has come about. New technologies have fundamentally altered our conceptions of space and time. Transatlantic air travel has made London accessible from New York in less than four hours by Concorde jet.

A sports fan can watch the Olympic Games by satellite in Rio de Janeiro at the very same time that a spectator is watching the actual competition taking place in Los Angeles. A document drawn up in Brussels now reaches Chicago by facsimile machine in less than five minutes.

Alvin Toffler, in his book *The Third Wave*, classifies human history in terms of three waves of radical change. He writes that:

Until now the human race has undergone two great waves of change, each one obliterating earlier cultures or civilizations and replacing them with ways of life inconceivable to those who came before. The First Wave of Change—the agricultural revolution—took thousands of years to play itself out. The Second Wave—the rise of industrial civilization—took a mere three hundred years. Today history is even more accelerative, and it is likely that the Third Wave will sweep across history and complete itself in a few decades. We, who happen to share this planet at this explosive moment, will therefore feel the full impact of the Third Wave in our own lifetimes.[4]

There is every reason to believe that the rapid evolution of society will continue in the near future—at least in the industrialized countries—and that the Second Industrial Revolution may have implications more monumental than those of the First Industrial Revolution. For example, the adversarial relationship that has characterized relations between workers and managers may dissolve as joint decisionmaking and profit-sharing come about. And it may turn out to be an age in which class differences in society abate as economic productivity becomes sufficient to effectively eliminate scarcities in goods and services.

Against this backdrop, a new equilibrium with respect to underlying structures could come about—a Modern Equilibrium that will allow for new economic and social stability and that may eventually bring about a new level of human civilization.

Traditional Equilibrium cannot be restored, particularly given modern communications and transport. But I am convinced that another period of global stability can be achieved. Just as all the primary material needs of the individual were met under Traditional Equilibrium, so, too, it may be possible to meet the material needs of the individual in Modern Equilibrium—though at an incomparably higher level of comfort and prosperity.

The here and now is a period between Traditional and Modern Equilibrium. The time period between the two equilibriums—the present—therefore defines the beginning and the end of the development process, which is characterized by flux and instability. At the heart of the problems facing development planners are the nature of the two fundamental changes in the world's socio-economic realities created by the First Industrial Revolution. One is humanity's irreparable break with Traditional Equilibrium. The second is the gradual and unanticipated creation of the distinct worlds of the rich and of the poor, which is a result of the fact that the Inter-Equilibrium phase did not begin simultaneously all over the world.

The developed and developing worlds have mutually affected each other. The development of the industrialized nations gathered momentum in part by maintaining and thus prolonging the traditional equilibrium of the colonies. Therefore, the gap started growing at that time and continued to do so even after the disappearance of imperialism for reasons which have been explained in the first chapter. Thus, today global dualism has become a worldwide problem. One of the chief aims of development must be the reintegration under Modern Equilibrium of the developed and developing worlds into a single human condition.

THE EMERGENCE OF UNDERDEVELOPMENT

Traditional Equilibrium was not a period of rampant hunger or permanent poverty. Agricultural production was limited to the cultivation of minimal food needs and little more, but, in the main, it was able to sustain communities throughout this age. Because it was dependent on natural conditions, it was vulnerable to disasters such as floods and droughts, but those were the exception, not the rule. Although the economic system under Traditional Equilibrium was simple, characterized by subsistence agriculture, production was often more than adequate to feed traditional societies.

The dawning of the new age brought numerous changes that, to a large extent, defined the future of most countries. For example, with colonialism came plantation agriculture. All development efforts and infrastructure were concentrated on the few crops slated for export and profit, such as rubber, palm oil, sugar, coffee, tea, and so on. The colonial administration supported mainly the efforts of plantation agriculture, and traditional subsistence farming was neglected; as a result the productivity of major food crops remained low. Regrettably, after independence, the governments of the former colonies continued the policies of the colonial powers. As a result, the economies of these countries, sustained to a considerable extent by a few export crops, are vulnerable to market fluctuations governing these products. Natural rubber, for example, has been largely replaced by cheaper and better quality synthetic rubber. As a result, the cultivation of rubber as one of Sri Lanka's most important export commodities reflects poorly in the nation's gross national product, since income from rubber is steadily falling. Similar distortions in Sri Lanka's production structures can also be traced to other measures established by the British colonial system.

Colonialism also brought about changes in the way native societies worked and produced. The extraction of mineral resources, the construction of ports, and the creation of urban centers in these nations changed what had formerly been a diffuse constellation of family plots and small town centers and, of course, resulted in large movements of labor to urban areas with a minimum of planning. In those cases where planning had been attempted by the colonial regimes, it was geared toward maximizing the productivity and profitability of imperial interests, and not toward enhancing the welfare of the native peoples.

One of the major features of the relationship between industrialized and less developed nations in the aftermath of the Industrial Revolution was an increasing dependency of the latter on the former. Mabogunje, describing one aspect of the dependency syndrome afflicting Third World countries today, speaks of colonialism as having denied

the African not only the opportunity of acquiring modern productive skills for processing the produce of his farms, forests and mines but also the chance of learning organizational skills needed for ensuring the smooth flow and delivery of these produce to foreign markets. . . .[5]

The Europeans brought education, medical care, and mechanical equipment to the colonies, but they did not pass on essential skills and knowledge to the indigenous populations. So when the stage was set for the independence of former imperial possessions, the indigenous leadership found their countries poor in human resources and unable to mobilize from among their own people the skills and experience needed to sustain the structure left by the colonial powers or to build, develop, and protect modern, independent states.

Generalizing and sustaining development in the poor nations of the world would be far easier if not for the problem of acute overpopulation. Not only are the population bases of these countries far larger than they were in the industrialized nations when the economic growth process began there, but the rate of population increase is far higher than at any other time in history. As a result of the population explosion, production structures are unable to meet primary needs, social existence has become extremely precarious in these countries—and the situation is continuing to deteriorate. Therefore, development economics must deal with a host of unprecedented phenomena.

It is possible to contend that even though consumption increases as population does, so, too, does production capacity, since, presumably, the number of workers in the labor force also increases. This reasoning is however negated by reality. The greater the natural increase in population, the higher is the number of consuming nonproducers, since children do not contribute to the economic system for some years after birth. Therefore, although production and productivity must rise at a rate commensurate with that of population increase to avoid shortfalls in meeting primary needs, because of constraints on capital, technology, and expertise, most Third World nations are unable today to raise their productivity on the required scale.

Labor mobility, a prerequisite of economic growth, can also create problems.[6] The population factor alone creates a great divergence between development realities as they existed early in the industrialized nations and as they exist today for the developing nations. As a result, I have concluded that full utilization of labor resources in the agricultural sector of developing societies, especially in the initial periods, is imperative.

One example of the critical importance of full employment in the agricultural sector can be seen in a regional development plan proposed for the Chaing Rai *Changwat* (province) of northern Thailand.[7] In 1971, Chaing Rai had a population of 1.1 million out of Thailand's 35 million inhabitants. A predominantly rural region, only 3 percent of the total population lived in the two preexisting small towns in Chaing Rai, and 83 percent of the total labor force was employed in agriculture. The per capita product of Chaing Rai in 1971 was $91 as compared with $185 for Thailand as a whole. The plan conceived for the province's development envisioned stepping up the rate of economic growth in the region in order to reduce the gap in living standards between the region and the country and eliminate the cause of out-migration from the region to the area of Bangkok.

According to population forecasts, by 1981 the population of Chaing Rai would reach 1.5 million, and the labor force would grow from 562,000 to 705,000. The planners thus made full employment of 705,000 people by the year 1981 one of their major goals. The plan was also designed to eliminate the underemployment that characterizes most of the agricultural labor force, due to the seasonality of rice cultivation. The main constraint facing the planners was the limited amount of resources that the Thai government could allocate to Chaing Rai.

In analyzing the relevant data, the planning team realized that if the trends of the past continued with no change in the percentage of the workers employed in agriculture, the *absolute gap* in per capita product between the region and the country as a whole would grow from $94 to $182, and the national per capita product in 1981 would reach $288, while that of the region would be as low as $106. Consequently, the planning team aimed at a modest goal of reducing the gap between regional and national per capita GNP in 1981 by 5 percent relative to the 1971 figures by achieving full employment of the agricultural labor in the region. An additional problem in attaining this goal was the expectation that by 1981, 11 percent of the peasantry would have been displaced from agriculture if no changes were made in the agricultural sector. Therefore, the plan concentrated on diversifying agriculture by including a second crop, introducing cattle husbandry and poultry raising, and establishing an expanded industrial and service production base using agricultural products. In changing the production structure of the region's agriculture, productivity of labor was increased, and underemployment was reduced by involving laborers left idle after the rice season in the cultivation of other crops, cattle rearing, and industrial activities. While this program would only gradually decrease the gap between the region and the nation in terms of per capita GNP, by fully utilizing the available labor the minimal needs of the population could be met in the long run, and the growing underdevelopment of the region arrested. Unfortunately, changes in the regime of that country precluded the implementation of the plan in its totality, although some of its features were later introduced.

The explosive urbanization and concomitant out-migration from rural areas that have taken place in the developing nations create a major problem for these societies. One of the major challenges faced by the development planner is the nature and size of metropolitan areas in developing nations. While only one-fourth of the people in the developing countries live in urban areas,[8] the rapidity with which Third World cities came about as well as their size, structure, and poverty are troublesome.

As Kuklinski and Petrella wrote: "Urbanization and industrialization are so closely linked with each other that it is hardly possible to think of the one without thinking of the other."[9] This identification of urbanization with industrialization has led to the mistaken notion that the growth of urban areas in developing nations has led to the expansion of industry and, ipso facto, to economic growth. Industrialization does not necessarily lead to economic growth; moreover, urbanization has had many negative consequences, including the spawning of unmanageable shanty towns and tent cities, pervasive unemployment, acute housing shortages, and especially rising crime rates.[10]

Perhaps the most telling of all the characteristics of urban proliferation in developing nations is described by Finkel:

Urbanization is a result of either a push or pull. The trend of urban migration is a universal phenomenon in all countries, but for different reasons.

There is . . . a group of reasons, which I would call negative—not the attraction of the town but the repulsion of the rural scene. There are people in many countries who leave the rural scene for the towns knowing that there is nothing awaiting them in town.

Yet they do not leave because they have become unnecessary. They leave because the farm standard of living is intolerable in every sense of the word. They work from dawn to dusk, with most of the profit going to the trader, the middleman. They see well-produced crops rotting because the marketing system is inadequate. They see the other ills of underdeveloped farming, of which we are constantly aware.

They go to the city for negative reasons. When you have a situation of this kind there is no symbiosis between urbanization and agricultural development. The people living close to starvation levels in the city do not increase the demand for farm products.[11]

Urban areas have always attracted labor by offering opportunities for economic livelihood to displaced agricultural workers. In the past, such workers would have greatly preferred to have remained in the villages while enjoying their accustomed pattern of life with its strong family ties. Today, not only do workers reject the rural life, but the levels of income needed to sustain a family in a developing country are more than can be derived from traditional farming. As a result of the population explosion, family plots have become ever more fragmented and smaller, and years of population pressure have also resulted in the deterioration of land resources. Thus the migration of rural labor to the cities is more likely a function of a "push" out of an insufferable rural predicament rather than of the "pull" or attraction of urban areas.

In starting their development later than did the industrialized nations, the developing countries face new problems that the industrialized countries never had to deal with. Overpopulation has depleted natural resources, and basic needs cannot be met without greatly straining the economic systems of these nations; moreover, the industrialized nations were not forced to deal with social problems at the same time development was taking place.

Urbanization in the developed countries had taken place gradually over the course of a century and a half hand in hand with the development of industry; in the developing countries this process has come about within three decades in the form of a spontaneous explosive urbanization. The result has been sheer chaos rather than development. The urban areas have assumed the semblance of urban society without receiving the material benefits that industrialized societies obtained as a result of their urbanization.

"Overurbanization" has been well described and analyzed by development specialists. For example, McGee notes in his book *The Urbanization Process in the Third World* that:

the form of the urbanization process in the Third World may appear to be the same as that which characterized the West, . . . however, the different *mix* of the components of the urbanization process in the Third World suggests that this factor is of such importance that at least one element of Western theory should be discarded when investigating the Third World city. This is the view that the city is an inducer of change [12]

This contention is true for a number of reasons, the most pressing one being that geographical mobility from rural to urban areas in developing countries has led to an unbalanced and socially dangerous structure in these cities. The permanent residents of Cairo, Tehran, Manila, Baghdad, Jakarta, Bangkok, Caracas, Quito, and Rio de Janeiro are not, for the most part, natives of the cities. The same holds true for virtually all metropolitan areas in Third World countries. Each of these cities can be divided into two distinct spheres, a micro-level, dualistic system. One of the urban spheres is equipped with most of the city's amenities and services and is home to the nation's elites. E. Brutzkus mentions the preference for extravagance in the construction and maintenance of private projects and the great attention paid to the areas in which the elites reside and projects undertaken for the sake of status on behalf of the elites.[13] The other sphere, which comprises the unplanned sprawling areas of urban blight, is devoid of most services, including in many instances electrification, potable water, transportation facilities, and sewage outlets. The "shanty towns" have one common denominator: they are the resident quarters of newcomers and other inhabitants who are among the poorest in the country.

The result is a polarization of twin and opposite cities throughout the developing world. H. Stretton has summarized the situation in his evaluation of urban planning in the poor countries:

Governments build grand quarters for themselves in their cities. They encourage private investments in central city offices, hotels, hospitals, affluent residential quarters with western standards of space and service, national and international airlines and airports, and fast motorways from the airports to the city centres. This sort of development is sometimes defended as creating conditions which will attract foreign businessmen and therefore further their investment—though any further investment it attracts is quite likely to be of the same unequalizing kind.[14]

In the developing world, urbanization is the result of the "push" rather than the "pull" to real jobs because of the transfer of high technology, capital-intensive, low-labor factories from the developed world. This kind of "transplanted" industrial development is limited in scope and utilizes mostly skills acquired by the more educated early residents of the city. The unskilled migrants in the developing countries turn to the service sector for employment. Such unskilled work is generally poorly rewarded in terms of wages and benefits. Therefore, the gap between the elites and the urban poor in developing countries is continuously increasing.

Geographical mobility not only affects the migrants; it also has many consequences that bode ill for the village. For example, a greater number of women, children, and the aged are mobilized on the land to compensate for the losses of male emigrant productive labor, which plays havoc with many aspects of village life. Education and the well-being of senior citizens fall victim to emigration from the rural village.[15] Another means used to fill the void left by those who have emigrated from the village is the mechanization of the large and medium-sized farms. What often results from rural mechanization, however, is a new socioeconomic gap within the village. Selective mechanization, as an essential element in the modernization process of agriculture, may be justified, but indiscriminate and premature adoption creates a growing gap between a rural elite and the mass of small farmers, with a consequent further erosion of village stability.

The village that has lost its youngest and generally most capable members becomes "old" very quickly. The birthrate declines (while rising dramatically in inner-city slums), and infant mortality rates remain high.[16] Concurrently, the village undergoes radical changes in its social composition.[17] Out-migration may even deplete the village's financial resources because of the need to support emigrant offspring who, due to the lack of opportunities in the cities, cannot meet their basic living expenses. As we shall see in greater detail later, a further irony of the situation is that the opposite often occurs as well: rural out-migrants will inadvertently tax the social fabric of their home villages by sending cash and gifts to their families, thereby creating new stratifications in those communities.

A United Nations study indicates that, if the trends of the past two decades persist, 62 percent of the world population will be urbanized by the year 2000, compared with the 38 percent of the population that currently inhabit urban areas in industrialized nations. This projected pattern of urbanization represents a worsening, not an improvement, in the development status of Third World countries. Against this backdrop, the reply of Flores to the rhetorical question, "Where is it more convenient for the Third World unemployed to go, in the country or in the city? In the country, of course," is a concise statement of the direction development activity must assume.[18] Urbanization in developing nations must be recognized as a sign of decay and deterioration, not as a symbol of progress.

The developing nations should not try to emulate the industrialized nations, whose present way of life is far from idyllic. The recognition that urbanization has inflicted tremendous harm on values systems and family cohesion implies that this is a major problem that the development effort must aim at rectifying.

THE PRIORITY OF VALUES IN DEVELOPMENT

The development specialist dealing with the conditions leading to economic growth must induce controlled change, taking into account the effects of any changes on values, which often means controlling intervention. Unfortunately, the preservation of values systems and their role in development has not received the attention it warrants. Even when values have been dealt with in the literature, the role of traditional values systems and kinship patterns have often been referred to in disparaging terms. For example, J. Kahl, in his *The Measurement of Modernism*, states that:

Traditional values . . . call for fatalistic acceptance of the world as it is, respect for those in authority, and submergence of the individual in collectivity. In contrast [m]odern values are rational and secular, permit choices and experiment, glorify efficiency and change, and stress individual responsibility.[19]

Kahl's glorification of modern values and his attack on traditional ones express one extreme in the spectrum of opinions on the subject. On the opposite end of the spectrum are those who maintain a reactionary view of values that interprets modern values as antithetical to God, *patria*, or morality.

In adopting one view or another with respect to the role traditional values systems and communities are to play in development, an apparent conflict emerges between advocacy of tradition as opposed to the modernizing effect of economic growth. The Brandt report states that "It is now widely recognized that development involves a profound transformation of the entire economic and social structure"[20] of a society, but I have long believed that development specialists must respect the traditional values of any developing society. This, of course, has led to my examining the appropriate level of intervention to be taken with respect to the values dimension of societal life. Finding the answer is one of the most difficult problems confronting decisionmakers attempting to formulate a policy of socioeconomic change in Third World countries.

In attempting to arrive at such a policy, the development planner must begin with an analysis of economic growth.

The first goal of economic growth is to provide primary material needs to the population, for no society can hope to industrialize or automate its economy if it cannot feed and shelter and educate its citizens. Since agriculture is the main economic sector of Third World countries, and is necessary to meeting the first goal, it plays a critical role in the development process. The potential contributions of agriculture to the economy are: increasing the food supply, providing productive work to a rapidly increasing rural population, creating capital for investment, and supporting industrial development.

However, most farmers in the developing countries are still producing at subsistence level. Because of the population explosion, labor is generally far in excess of productive labor opportunities in agriculture. As a result, agriculture produces barely enough for survival and cannot make a substantial contribution to economic growth. Thus countries in which the majority of the population is engaged in subsistence agriculture, and which have no other important natural resources, are inevitably poor, with stagnant economies.

Until recently, agriculture in the developing countries has been neglected by policymakers, economists, and development planners, on the assumption that all available resources should be involved in industrial development. Experience has, however, shown that overall development is not likely to occur unless agricultural productivity is increased as a prelude to industrial growth—in other words, unless a transformation of traditional agriculture takes place.

For a number of reasons, the developing nations must generate the resources necessary to provide their citizens with the necessities of life by themselves. The means employed in achieving this goal must be labor-intensive rather than capital-intensive for two reasons: (a) the amount of capital needed to meet the material needs of the population in these nations is astronomical, and (b) employment opportunities are limited. To ensure that the immense resources necessary at this stage are available, government interventions are necessary. The mix of development forces at this stage must favor the needs of the society as a whole, as opposed to those of any other privileged sector. Consequently, the values systems of developing societies in this stage of economic growth must provide for the kind of social order that is a necessary prerequisite to the mobilization of national resources. The governmental authorities responsible for development must be provided with all the power necessary to fulfill their responsibilities.

In the next stage of economic growth, with the economic system improved enough to meet the primary food, clothing, and housing needs of the population, the challenge for society becomes the expansion of its production capacity so that scarcities of goods and services can be reduced. At this point, the development campaign should struggle to improve the capacity of the national "center to transfer human and capital resources to the rest of the national territory."[21] This will require the elimination of most of the discrepancies between various sectors of the nation.

This stage of development involves the reallocation of production capacity, resources, occupational structures, and services throughout the national space so that the divergencies between rural and other regions of the country are reduced. For reasons inherent to the economic system at this stage of development, the best way to redistribute national resources involves, besides reallocation, the expansion of production capacity and the improvement of productivity. Therefore, in the middle stages of economic growth, in order to further expansion of productive capacity, private interests should be given the facilities required to fully develop their intrinsic economic strength. Accordingly, at this stage, public intervention in the economic system should be confined to redistributing national resources and preempting any exploitative trends displayed by private interests. Individuals should be encouraged to maximize their contribution to the economic system, whether through profits, prestige, leadership privileges, or other incentives.

If all goes well to this point, I believe that in the next stage of economic growth, another and deeper transformation in social values takes place. When production capacity increases dramatically, the income gaps between different socioeconomic classes will gradually close. This last stage, which is the one the nations of the world have yet to enter, is the final stage of the Inter-Equilibrium phase preceding Modern Equilibrium. If the needs of all individuals in society will be met and an abundance of goods and services will eliminate economic concerns as the primary determinant of human relations, toward the end of this stage and throughout Modern Equilibrium, a natural balance will come about between the individual and society. The two forces will engage each other in a dialectic in which each will check the influence of the other. In other words, during Modern Equilibrium the power and influence of society will be aimed solely at preventing the exploitation of the public good by individual interests. At the same time, individuals must prevent the excessive and undue intervention of government in the private affairs of the population.

The balancing of societal and individual aspirations will constitute the function of social values under Modern Equilibrium. This may sound strange to those living in a materialistic culture in which social relations are governed by the vagaries of the economic struggle. Because humanity has been grappling since the dawn of history with the need for material survival and the allocation of scarce necessities, imagination may fail to comprehend what may lie in store for the fully affluent society of the future.

Although each of the stages of economic growth requires some degree of modification in values systems, this is not a license to trample on values systems. For the development planner today, the preservation of values systems that are compatible with the economic requirements of development should be an end in itself.

THE PRIORITIES OF DEVELOPMENT

The developing countries, comprising more than two-thirds of humanity, are in dire need of a new model for development. In this book, written in the pursuit of such a model, I will endeavor to describe a general strategy for economic growth in the developing countries, a suitable system of social values that will support and even propel the economy forward, and a means for preserving the basic values of those societies while doing so. My theory is based on the premise that the developing world should progress in three stages, or periods (see the table below).

It is basically a new model of development, one that does not resemble the model used by the industrialized nations.

In the first and immediate stage, provision must be made for meeting primary economic needs while creating a social balance between the government and the individual. It will require understanding of the basic values in society that stem from tradition.

Once the first stage of development is achieved, the process will continue into the second stage, during which economic growth is propelled by the forces of social competition. The system of social values will guarantee individual freedom and the balance vis-a-vis necessary societal restrictions. All efforts will be made to conserve and preserve the system of basic values. This will, in due course, bring the poor countries of today to the stage of economic affluency enjoyed at present by the rich countries, while avoiding the bitter struggle and controversies over social values that Western civilization has endured since the First Industrial Revolution. It will also serve to bolster the basic values of the masses in these societies and preserve them for the full affluence of the future.

Once the developing countries reach the second stage, they will be ready to enter into the world created by the Second Industrial Revolution. They, too, will be able to make full use of automation and computerization in all spheres of human activity and be affluent enough for each individual to give according to his capability and receive all that he requires.

When the third stage is reached by all the nations of the world,

Table 2-1: The Three Stages of Development and Their Components

Components	First Stage	Second Stage	Third Stage
Economic Growth	Assuring "primary needs"	Social competition	Full affluency
Social Values	Social balance	Individual freedom	Meaningless
Basic Values	Continuation of past tradition	Conserving the system	Fully supportive

the system of basic values will enhance and strengthen the individual's meaningful and peaceful way of life, shielding him from the corrosive power of doubt, nihilism, escapism, and despair. I believe that at that stage, man will have made possible, for each individual, what that individual will consider "the good life."

CHAPTER 3

ECONOMIC STRUCTURES AND THE DEVELOPMENT FRAME OF REFERENCE

Confusion about the intrinsic nature of economic growth, its internal dynamics, and the manner in which it can be measured has always hampered efforts to formulate a suitable program for Third World development. The standards employed in determining whether or not an economic system has in fact improved or deteriorated are not clear; yet standards against which to gauge the relative development of a specific society are essential for instituting economic change. If an adequate conceptualization of the economic growth process were available, it would be possible to formulate an analytic framework to use in constructing a useful frame of reference for development. It is important, therefore, to review the conventional views of economic growth and to assess what, if any, insight they offer into the growth process and the means to stimulate it.

CONCEPTUALIZING ECONOMIC GROWTH

While there is little consensus in today's development literature about what constitutes economic growth, there is widespread dissatisfaction with the conventional form of economic growth measurement represented by the per capita gross national product (GNP). Lowdon Wingo states that the GNP index is

a measure with serious defects. GNP is the sum of nonhomogeneous productive events which . . . needs to be disaggregated into distinguishable, interregional economic relations that can be separately evaluated.[1]

As an indicator of economic change, the per capita GNP is limited because it measures change from one year to the next in the production output of a nation examined as a whole, ignoring changes in production capacity and the efficiency of production systems. The per capita GNP does not consider the way in which increases in national product are distributed between regions and within them, nor does it account for the poor distribution of income and resources between nations. Similarly, it does not reveal how increases in the national product came about or indicate the internal strengths and weaknesses of the economic system.

Although different theorists have presented different analyses of economic growth, development specialists have not accepted any of them as either comprehensive or authoritative. But while these proposals concerning economic analysis are, in my view, incorrect, they offer insights that further the search for an analytic framework for development economics.

One of the most debated studies in development economics is Walt W. Rostow's *The Stages of Economic Growth: A Non-Communist Manifesto*. Rostow's theory envisions five stages in the development process: (1) traditional society, (2) preconditions for take-off into self-sustained growth, (3) take-off, (4) the drive to maturity, and (5) the age of high mass consumption. Even though Rostow's evolutionary stage theory has been challenged because it is not rooted in empirical, statistical analysis, it still made a contribution: it was the first attempt to generalize the process of development and attribute to it certain regularity and stages.

In contrast, Simon Kuznets's study *Economic Growth of Nations* is rooted in empirical analysis;[2] like a number of others in the same vein, it correlates the per capita GNP with several socioeconomic variables for a number of developed countries. Among the indicators are the relationship between rates of growth and increased productivity in the yearly national product, as well as shifts in the structure of production. Implicit in Kuznets's analysis is the notion that the more developed an economic system is, the higher the share of industry and services in its GNP and the lower the percentage share of agriculture both in its GNP and in the labor force. The growth process in developed nations saw the share of the agricultural sector in the GNP drop from 40 to 10 percent, while the industrial sector in the GNP rose from between 22 and 25 percent to between 40 and 90 percent, with a concomitant, albeit modest rise in the share of services.

Kuznets believes that the inverse relationship between agriculture and industry in the GNP and the work force is the result of the high rate of shift in the structures of preference (demand for manufactured goods increases as the economic system provides primary material needs to the population). The shift, in turn, brings about an increase in demand for manufactured goods, which increases profitability for those involved in manufacturing, changing the advantage in investing from agriculture to industry. Finally, because of the high selectivity of technological innovations, there are shifts from one branch of production to another.[3]

Irma Adelman and Cynthia Taft Morris studied growth by analyzing social, economic, and political variables in seventy-four developing countries between 1950 and 1964.[4] The variables associated with economic growth that they analyzed were: (1) the process of change in attitudes and institutions associated with the breakdown of traditional social organization; (2) the variation in political systems among countries; (3) the character of leadership (strength of the traditional elite and degree of administrative efficiency); and (4) the degree of social and political stability necessary for development.

Their contribution to a suitable understanding of economic growth lies in their realization that noneconomic factors impinge, both positively and negatively, on development. In essence, they found that an absolute rise in national product in developing countries does not necessarily translate into any improvement, and may in fact mark a deterioration, in the plight of the nation's poor. Therefore, growth cannot be described in terms of increased national product alone; it must also refer to the distribution of the national product.

The International Labor Organization (ILO) has studied growth in terms of the relative increases or decreases in the allocation of primary material needs—food, education, and housing, among others—achieved for the society as a whole. However, this approach records increases and decreases for an entire nation rather than within the nation—the spatial aspect of development.

Different formulas for indexing distribution have been proposed. Among these are proposals seeking indicators of the quality of life, of efficiency in producing goods and services, and of the allocation of the benefits of economic growth among different strata of the society. Some approaches to the measurement of change in the quality of life include: (a) examinations of fluctuations in the amount of leisure time in a society and (b) composite indices, composed of indicators for various socioeconomic phenomena, including the "Level of Living" or "Development Index" proposed by the United Nations Research Institute for Social Development (UNRISD)[5] or the "Physical Quality of Life Index" offered by David Morris and the Overseas Development Council.[6] All such proposals for measuring the quality of life through composite indices present a major difficulty: what priority should be ascribed to each socioeconomic indicator?[7] Should the industrial share in the GNP be considered equal to the number of health clinics available in rural areas? Is the number of clinics more important than the number of primary schools?

Earlier approaches to economic growth that included social as well as economic indicators failed to adequately address the distributional component of economic growth. Hollis B. Chenery et al. have created a formula whereby the growth rates displayed by developing societies were adjusted in terms of different weights attached to various strata in the society. For example, if a lower strata showed an improvement in income, this was weighed more heavily than an improvement in income level of the upper strata. But Chenery's formulation does not provide a means of deciding when a relatively small income increase among lower strata should— or should not—be more heavily weighed than a large increase in income among the better-off. For example, is a per capita improvement of $50 for the poorest classes in the society socially more constructive than a per capita $1,000 increase for the middle class?

Somewhat more satisfactory proposals along the same lines are offered by Anthony Barnes Atkinson[8] and Serge Christophe Kolm,[9] who both suggest indices that measure the level of total income that, if equally distributed throughout the society, would give all strata the same level of welfare that derive from the present unequal income distribution.

These approaches all contribute to the search for an understanding of the growth process. But even if the positive points made by these approaches are combined, they will not describe fully how economic resources can be satisfactorily and effectively distributed among the various sectors of the population.

Historically, conventional economics has conceived of two spheres in economic systems: macroeconomics, dealing with the overall production activities of a society, and microeconomics, addressing the patterns of production and consumption by individuals in society. These two spheres are regarded as being mutually autonomous: changes in the production and consumption structures are viewed as affecting each other only in terms of supply and demand.

Virtually all conventional approaches to economic growth can be viewed as belonging to one of two categories: (1) studies that measure and describe economic growth on the basis of national production averages and, therefore, describe growth as seen from the panoramic view of the nation and (2) those that concentrate on the consumption patterns exhibited by individuals. For those studies dealing with the macro-perspective, both the production and distributional aspects of growth are described by indicators that have significance only if the society is taken as an economically homogeneous entity. The micro-perspective, on the other hand, employs concepts, such as that of primary material needs, which have meaning only on the level of the individual. Similarly, income distribution assumes an entirely different significance from an individual viewpoint: while society may show an increase in the GNP from one year to the next, no such increase, and even a net decrease, may be found among a numerically large strata of the society.

The fundamental problem with all of the approaches previously offered by development economists is rooted in their neglect of the spatial dimension of economic growth. Morgan D. Thomas writes in this connection that:

Economic theory has contributed very little to the explanation of spatial distribution of economic activities. This situation is unfortunate because such explanations are needed if we are to solve some important practical contemporary economic problems—for example, the planning problem of determining the optimum, or most desirable, dispersion of economic activity to achieve a particular rate of economic growth for a selected region.[10]

The changes brought about by economic growth must be analyzed from the standpoint of the transformation manifested over both time and space. The temporal dimension in economic growth addresses increases in income and productivity, but it fails to contend with distribution. The spatial dimension is concerned with the expansion of production capacity and services, as well as with the distribution of preexisting and new levels of wealth throughout all strata on all levels. As Mennes, Tinbergen, and Waardenburg state: "By the introduction of space, the main problem of development planning acquires an additional dimension."[11] Both dimensions are integral to the economic growth process.

THE STRUCTURES OF ECONOMIC GROWTH

In formulating my own Development Frame of Reference, a device that is meant to bring development specialists closer to the kind of planning that will bring about equitable economic growth, it was necessary to try to understand both the temporal and spatial structural changes that growth brings about.[12] The spatial dimension deals with the aggregation of resources and production capacity from the point of view of national and regional conglomerations of production units. It also deals with the disaggregation of resources and production capacity and indicates their distribution on the local level of the production unit. The evolution of changes over time is divisible into stages (which were tabulated in Chapter 2), and the significance of each growth stage is different for each spatial level of functioning.

With the recognition that economic growth takes place in two dimensions, efforts to arrive at a suitable conception of the growth process must deal with the different correlations for each stage of growth* at each societal level. The national level is the aggregation of all production units existing in the national economy. In contrast, each individual production unit has a multiplicity of characteristics.

The essential differences between economic growth in these dimensions are related to the way in which economic growth is structured at each level. For example, an Israeli planning team cooperating with planners on the El-Sisal development project in

---

*Stages of growth are presented herein as a heuristic concept. That is, for the purposes of analysis and planning, the development process can be treated as occurring in stages.

the Dominican Republic[13] found that the introduction of water siphons in irrigation sharply increased the productivity of peasant farmplots and had a dramatic effect on local production structures. The introduction of this simple device in production technology had only a marginal effect on national productivity; in order to have a national impact, the technological advances would have to spread to a multiplicity of production units. Changes in production, though, are not introduced and activated simultaneously.

The scale of the individual production unit is such that a technological innovation affects all aspects of the farm family's life; by improving the family's productivity, innovation raises its standard of living. The spatial extent of the nation, however, is such that the diffusion of technology moves slowly from one farm to another and from one region to another—national growth, while continuous over the long run, takes time.

Economic growth presents itself differently at each societal level at any given point in time. The implications of this "time-space" relationship for planning are described by Nathaniel Lichtfield:

[For any particular country] it is necessary to have some integration of national, regional and local planning, for otherwise there can be no coordination between the socioeconomic and physical . . . dimensions. Such an approach could clearly best be made within the framework of comprehensive planning at all levels. By this is meant planning that is carried out at the national, regional and local level, with a comprehensive approach to the meaning of development in its economic, social and physical terms. This includes the planning process, which is geared to the needs and possibilities of action through development and where the implementation process is as important as the planning process itself and the use of physical development for community development is as important as both.[14]

In a Development Frame of Reference* the temporal and spatial dimensions of economic growth must be considered and correlated. For example, four stages in the growth process characterize the transformation of the farm: subsistence, diversified, specialized,

---

*For a fuller explanation of the Development Frame of Reference and its stages, see Raanan Weitz, *From Peasant to Farmer* (New York: Columbia University Press, 1971).

and automated. The changing production attributes over time for each stage are presented in Table 3-1, which shows the temporal and spatial development for the farm, a single production unit. A similar set of temporal-spatial changes also occurs in industrial and service production units. National economic growth in the industrial and service sectors is similar to growth in the agricultural sector. At the level of the individual production unit in agriculture, industry, and service, the structural changes appear as jumps from one stage of development to another. But when viewed from the macro level of the region or of the nation, such technological changes are continual and gradual. What is observed depends on the viewer's capacity to discern aggregative detail.

In differentiating the four levels of societal functioning, the national level can be defined as the total aggregate of productive activity and output taking place on the individual level. The regional level is slightly more complicated in that a distinction must be made between the metropolitan and the rural areas. To a certain extent, the distinction is arbitrary. But, since Third World societies today are polarized into two distinct spheres, it is an important distinction—and one that is essential for planning purposes:

A primate i.e. metropolitan city distribution is one in which the settlement pattern consists of only two main ranks. The city on the one hand and the village and small rural town on the other. This leads to a severe dichotomy. The cities tend to grow and develop, becoming showcases of modernity, where the rich and capable center and investment is attracted. The rural regions meanwhile, affording no opportunities and attractions for investment, tend to stagnate. With no know-how and cumbersome means of communications these regions remain cut-off from the outer world and the main stream of progress, thereby keeping living standards low.

Such a system is self-perpetuating, for the everpresent emigration from village to town having no place else to go, finds its way into the city, creating vast labor surplus and overcrowding. This makes the city an even more lucrative place for industries which are out for cheap labor and for land speculators who encourage slum formation.[15]

In planning development, a developing country should be regarded *as if* it were composed of one metropolitan center and a rural periphery. In practical terms, this means that the functional distinction is accounted for by formulating separate plans for the abstract "metropolitan region" (composed statistically of all large urban conglomerates in the country) and the "rural region" (composed statistically of all nonmetropolitan, i.e., rural, areas of the country). For computational purposes, the national level of societal functioning is defined as including both the metropolitan and rural regions. The rural region, for the purposes of calculation, is defined as the net averages for socioeconomic indicators on the national level minus the averages for the same indicators for the metropolitan region. A major objective of development is the reduction of the socioeconomic disparities between the metropolitan and rural regions.[16]

The planner who would use a tool such as the Development Frame of Reference must first understand the dynamics inherent in economic growth at all stages and levels of their coevolution. I began, therefore, by analyzing the main features of the growth process in terms of values computed for numerous indicators as they relate to a variety of countries at different stages of economic growth. This enabled me to correlate economic patterns with the stages in the growth process. The sampling I used was limited by the paucity of available development data, not only for the development nations but for the Western industrialized countries. Consequently, the "normative parameters" of past trends and future prospects cannot be regarded as statistically representative of all development situations and can be viewed as heuristic. My research was as empirically grounded as prevailing conditions allowed. While I do not claim scientific validity for it, the conclusions I derived, working closely with my Rehovot team as explained in the Preface, can serve as a basis of continuing development research and, most important, provide orientation for development planning and implementation.

My attempts to associate particular combinations of economic conditions with different rates of economic growth relied on the selection of suitable indicators. In large part, the selection of such indicators was preordained: the lack of consistent record-keeping in the past is ubiquitous in the developed and developing countries alike. Within these limitations, I chose indicators appropriate to each level of societal functioning. At the national level, I used indicators that register averages for the nation as an entity. To compute values for the rural region, the averages for the metropolitan area were subtracted from those for the national level. For the local level, given the direct and all-encompassing impact of

Table 3-1: Development and Structure of the Individual Farm Unit

Characteristics	Development Scale			
	Subsistence	Diversified	Specialized	Automated
The Individual Family Farm				
Farm Type	Subsistence	Diversified	Specialized	Automated
Farm Branches	Mainly staple	Varied livestock	Main branch and auxiliary	One branch
Product Destination	Home consumption	Marketing and home consumption	Marketing and processing	Mainly processing
Production Method	Traditional	Modern inputs	Capital-intensive	Highly sophisticated
Output Value ($)	300–1,000	2,000–6,000	10,000–30,000	Over 50,000
Ratio of Value Added per Output ($)	90–60	50–40	35–25	25 and less

Investment per Workday ($)	2–6	15–35	50–85	350–500
Added Value per Workday ($)	2–4	5–15	15–30	Over 35
Annual Work Schedule	Seasonal unemployment	Balanced	Depends on farm type	Mostly seasonal

The National Economy

Per Capita GNP ($)	120–450	600–2,800	2,800–5,000	Over 6,500
Gross Product (%)				
Agriculture	30–65	18–30	8–15	5–7
Industry	10–30	20–40	35–45	45–60
Services	20–40	40–50	40–50	50–60
Employment (%)				
Agriculture	50–80	20–45	8–18	40–45
Industry	5–20	20–35	35–40	40–45
Services	15–30	40–50	45–50	50–60

economic change on the individual production unit, a large number of indicators were used to provide a detailed description of the individual production units in all three sectors.

My sources of empirical data included statistical information supplied by the World Bank and the UNRISD and data from the country profiles assembled by my colleagues at Rehovot. Pertinent statistical information concerning the development of the industrialized nations is generally available for the period since the 1920s and 1930s. By that time, though, the developed countries had fully absorbed the impact of the first industrial revolution, and having progressed out of the traditional and primary needs stage of growth, were well on their way toward social competition. The dearth of data concerning the early stages of development in these nations has made it difficult to measure the current status of development in the developing nations against the corresponding period in the developed countries. Another problem relating to the existing statistical information is the wide variety of methods by which data were garnered in the past within different countries. Also, many of the national, regional, and local agencies in both areas did not, and do not, collect information in a consistent, systematic, and standardized way.

Despite all of the problems with existing development data, it still has its uses:

the poverty of the data is an intrinsic condition of underdevelopment, not a happenstance. This is not to say, of course, that the available information should not be used. On the contrary, its very scarcity makes it especially valuable. . . . [T]he planner must put together and use his incomplete information as a detective puts together his fragmentary clues, using to his utmost his judgment and ingenuity to join formal data with any other information to produce indicators of the condition and performance of the socioeconomic system.[17]

The major countries profiled represent a spectrum of societies at different stages of development, where suitable information for specific time periods was available and reliable research institutions cooperated. This naturally means a limited sample, but I believe that when enhanced by years of personal firsthand experience in development planning, the sample can help show the way to a planning system based on the preliminary tools derived from the material with which I have worked. The sample contains poor, middle-income, and rich nations, but does not include nations from the Eastern European bloc. Nonetheless, these countries embody some of the major patterns underlying the development of nations at different stages of economic growth.

The institutions that cooperated provided information pertaining to the local, regional, and national levels of societal functioning. On the regional level, I sought data for both urban and rural areas. On the local level, I asked for statistics for a typical farm, industrial plant, and service unit (e.g., a school or clinic). The time period I was most interested in was the twenty-year span from the early 1950s to the mid-1970s. All information was dated, and the monetary figures were given in local currency, with the corresponding exchange rate for U.S. dollars at the time.

Generally, the information I was given was collected with care and entailed substantial effort on the part of the institutions that provided it. On the basis of the answers to questionnaires, I compiled a country profile for each nation cited, then after establishing the reliability of particular indicators and clarifying ambiguous figures, the relevant statistics were combined and classified.

Essentially, one set of indicators was applied to the national and regional levels, and another to the local level. Both sets of data, composed of mean averages for macro level phenomena (on the national and regional levels) and figures representing a "typical" local level entity, pertain to production structures in each sector and to the percentage maintained by each sector in the GNP and labor force. Other indicators relate to spatial differences in essential services, as between national and regional levels, and between the regional and local levels.

The indicators and the normative values derived for them, relating to the national and regional levels for the countries studied, are presented in the following table.

"Normative parameters" refer to calculations made for various indicators using the data collected from the World Bank, UNRISD, and the country profiles. As such, the normative parameters indicate normal ranges for the countries selected; they are not intended as definitive averages for all nations. Rather, they are intended to show the order of magnitude of patterns I found characteristic of the data base I studied. While subsequent research

Table 3-2: The Normative Parameters for the
National and Regional Levels of the Development Frame of Reference

Stage	Primary Needs		Social Competition		Full Affluency	
Indicators	National	Regional	National	Regional	National	Regional
Production Structure						
Agricultural Share in GDP (%)	15–30	22–38	10–15	15–25	3–6	5–10
Industrial Share in GDP(%)	15–20	5–10	35–45	30–36	35–45	35–48
Services Share in GDP (%)	35–50	32–50	48–52	38–50	50–60	50–55
Labor Force in Agriculture (%)	25–60	30–65	10–20	12–23	3–9	6–10
Labor Force in Industry (%)	20–30	15–20	35–40	30–36	35–45	35–47
Labor Force in Services (%)	25–40	25–30	40–50	38–50	50–60	48–55
International Trade (exports and imports) per Capita ($)	150–600	120–550	300–2,500	500–1,500	1,300–4,500	1,000–4,000
Demographic Situation						
Birth Rate per 1000 Births	20–34	12–37	12–20	12–22	10–16	10–16
Infant Mortality Rate per 1000 Births	35–120	45–130	10–18	10–20	8–16	8–16

Life Expectancy at Birth (in years)	73–76	75–78	72–75	72–75	45–55	57–65
Percentage of Urban Population	—	60–85	—	55–80	—	30–40
Income and Consumption						
Per Capita Income (%)	6,000–8,500	6,000–8,500	2,300–4,500	2,500–4,500	280–1,900	400–2,000
Food Consumption (% of total income)	18–20	18–20	28–35	22–30	40–60	27–40
Energy Consumption (kgs. of coal per capita)	not known	6,000–11,000	not known	2,500–6,000	not known	300–1,900
Social Indicators						
Size of Average Family	3–6	3–5	5–6	4–6	6–7	5–7
Rate of Illiteracy (%)	none	none	2–3	1–2	30–65	25–70
Population per Physician	400–600	400–600	400–1,000	400–900	10,000–20,000	2,000–15,000
Secondary Education (% of age group)	70–94	70–94	45–90	50–92	15–25	20–60
International Trade (exports and imports)						
Per Capita ($)	1,000–4,000	1,300–4,500	500–1,500	300–2,500	120–550	150–600

61

is needed to gather data for all countries and thereby determine with greater statistical precision the specific values that are normative for different societies, at different levels and different stages of the growth process, it is my opinion that the normative parameters can serve to guide planners in targeting growth goals. By correlating these parameters and associating combinations of them with particular development statuses, I have been able to prepare a Development Frame of Reference that can be used, albeit somewhat tentatively, to determine the relative development status of a society and to direct planning and implementation activities geared toward economic growth.

The normative parameters for the national and regional levels reveal strategically significant trends. When these two levels are compared, it becomes apparent that in the earlier stages of economic growth the differences between national and regional averages are always substantial, but they diminish as economic growth progresses (this, as explained earlier, is the outcome of the diminishing gap between the metropolitan center and the rural areas). When the nations arrive at the brink of the stage I call full affluency, the difference between the two levels tends to disappear. While at the earlier stages of economic growth there is a large gap in the number of industrial and service enterprises in the metropolitan center as opposed to rural areas, the gap tends to diminish and close completely as the country approaches the stage of full affluency. These general rules apply to the employment ratio between the three sectors—agriculture, industry, and services—as well as for the demographic, income, consumer, and social indicators.

Another important trend is found in the relative share in the GNP of the three main sectors. Initially, agriculture's share in the GNP is much lower than its share in the labor force, suggesting that agricultural production at this stage is inefficient because of deficiencies in the technology of production. At the present situation, agriculture's share in the labor force is 85 to 95 percent, while its share in the GNP is between 40 and 75 percent. When reaching the stage of primary needs, the economic situation of the developing countries should change and assume the indicators tabulated in Table 3-2. By the final stage approaching modern equilibrium, agriculture's shares in employment and the GNP are equal—between 3 and 6 percent—showing that labor, while reduced in terms of absolute and relative numbers of workers employed, is displaying maximum productivity and efficiency. This means that the income of the agricultural worker equals the average income of all wage-earners at both the regional and national levels. Differences between the national and regional averages in the percentage of those employed in industry and the services are even more significant. Initially, there are marked differences between industry in the metropolitan areas and in the rest of the country, which gradually disappear.

The picture that emerges is illuminating: the process of economic growth coincides with a progressive diffusion of the share of the fruits of economic growth throughout the nation. In the final stage, the average per capita incomes are the same for the metropolitan areas as for the rest of the country. The percentage of food and energy consumed as compared with total consumption undergoes the same process and, consequently, the social indicators improve.

The table also indicates clearly that one of the most important aspects of continuous economic growth is an ever-decreasing gap between metropolitan and rural areas. Of course, it is not clear whether the diffusion process is the cause or the outcome of economic growth. Is the gradual infiltration of non-agricultural activities from the metropolitan to the rural areas the catalyst for or the consequence of economic growth? Historically, industrialization and the development of services have been associated with urbanization. Therefore, the strategic direction of development must be toward the diffusion of industry and services throughout the country, rather than the concentration of these sectors in the cities.

Similar trends are revealed for the local level, which is logical given that any economic system depends on what happens in all units of production, including all sizes and sorts of farms, industrial enterprises, and the full gamut of services from those of public origin, such as government offices, to those that are totally private, such as retail shops. It is what actually happens daily in the units of production that ultimately shapes the national and regional economic systems. A clear and realistic picture of the local level cannot be drawn unless it includes those features that determine the nature and relationships of the individual production units. For this purpose, it is no longer possible to use average numbers representing macro activities and populations in a panoramic way. Rather, the main features of the economy must be reduced to a few representative indicators that characterize the main units of production in all three sectors.

Given the enormous ecological, sociological, and cultural diversity of individual production units, it is impossible to describe each with any detail. The main aim in trying to derive normative parameters for the local level is to discern and describe the most common denominators of some of the main types of production units. Therefore, agricultural units of production are presented and analyzed in terms of four types of farms: large extensive farms, small intensive farms, the most common farm, and the most advanced farm. In the industrial sector, I chose the most typical enterprises for the six main branches of industry: food, textiles, metal, chemical, electrical, and construction; in the service sector, nine kinds of service institutions: the primary school, secondary school, local clinic, hospital, grocery shop, community center, transportation company, bank, and local government office.

Tables 3-3 to 3-5 summarize the normative parameters for the countries in the data base. These tables comprise the proposed Development Frame of Reference on the local level at the three stages in the growth process.

The multi-level, evolutionary analysis of economic growth described above is at the core of the Development Frame of Reference. After analyzing the data in terms of the three stages of economic growth, I made normative correlations that produced patterns related not only to the GNP of a society but to other aspects of economics. For instance, the technology of production— namely the relationship according to which capital, material resources, and human labor are deployed—appears to be a critical factor in the economic growth of a society. While previous economic theorists have stressed the quantity of resources available to a society as the major determinant of economic growth, my research indicates that the manner in which resources are deployed is at least as important and perhaps more so than the quantity of capital and material resources available to a given economic system. Since relatively small quantities of capital and natural resources are now available to developing societies, and given the fact that human labor is the most abundant resource in these societies, it is essential for them to find the most productive way to utilize the human resource.

When the regional and local levels are compared, the difference in their *rates* of economic growth is fascinating. At the regional level the indicators show a rather gradual ascent, while the characteristics of the local units of production jump from one stage to another. This is evident, for example, when comparing the values of production at each stage of economic growth in the system as a whole on both the national and regional levels against the values of production output for the individual unit. Even when the values for the output of the units in all economic sectors leaped from one stage to another—sometimes by a factor of ten—this never happened at the national or regional levels.

The very size and weight of the national and regional levels in comparison to the local level causes economic growth on the former to take place slowly and continuously in contrast to the latter level where it takes place in jumps.

Another trend emerging from the differences between levels is the spatial configuration of agricultural production compared to that of the industrial sector. The normative parameters derived for the data base show that the location of various enterprises spreads from the center to the periphery, that is, from metropolitan to rural areas. The same is true for service institutions or organizations, although here the spread is expressed more by the size of the population served, rather than by its location. Combining the nature and structure of the farm brings the whole picture into sharp relief—the time and space dimensions produce one coherent framework.

THE DEVELOPMENT FRAME OF REFERENCE

While the countries selected for the data base are not regarded as *statistically* representative of the development process, I believe that the normative parameters established for them can be used to indicate the approximate direction of the growth process. The main purpose of the Development Frame of Reference is to correlate the normative parameters in one model of development continuity so that its strategic and tactical requirements can be viewed against a hypothetical evolutionary scale.

As will be explained in greater depth in Chapter 5, I analyzed the data in a number of ways to determine strategic goals of development, such as the maximization of labor power and the diffusion of technology, production capacity, and income from the

Table 3-3: Agricultural Farms:
The Normative Parameters for the Local Level of the Development Frame of Reference

Farm Type	Characteristics	Stages of Economic Growth		
		Primary Material Needs	Social Competition	Full Affluency
Large Extensive Farm	Cultivated area (hectares)	5	50	65.0
	Number of employed	12	3	2.5
	Value of output ($)	4,000	30,000	50,000
	Output per employee ($)	3,300	10,000	20,000
	Added value per employee ($)	2,300	7,000	12,000
Small Intensive Farm	Cultivated area (hectares)	1	7	7
	Number of employed	1	2	1
	Value of output ($)	2,550	20,000	9,000

Output per employee ($)	2,550	10,000	9,000
Added value per employee ($)	1,550	6,000	6,000
Most Common Farm			
Cultivated area (hectares)	2.0	35.0	35
Number of employed	1.5	2.5	1.6
Value of output ($)	4,500	36,000	27,000
Output per employee ($)	3,000	14,700	17,000
Added value per employee ($)	2,000	8,000	7,000
Most Advanced Farm			
Cultivated area (hectares)	—	0.8	0.5
Number of employed	—	1.8	1.7
Value of output ($)	—	40,000	60,000
Output per employee ($)	—	22,000	35,000
Added value per employee ($)	—	12,000	14,000

Table 3–4: Industrial Enterprises:
The Normative Parameters for the Local Level of the Development Frame of Reference

Industrial Type	Characteristics	Stages of Economic Growth		
		Primary Material Needs	Social Competition	Full Affluency
Food	Number of employed	50	120	130
	Output value (thousands)	750	3,000	4,800
	Output per employee (thousands)	15	25	37
	Added value per employee (thousands)	5	7	12
	Location	R	R	V
Textiles	Number of employed	60	70	125
	Output value (thousands)	480	840	2,300
	Output per employee (thousands)	8	12	18
	Added value per employee (thousands)	2.9	5.5	9
	Location	MT	RT	RT
Metals	Number of employed	50	200	550
	Output value (thousands)	400	6,000	24,600
	Output per employee (thousands)	8	30	44

Added value per employee (thousands)	3.9	12	20
Location	LT	LT	RT
Chemicals			
Number of employed	60	150	250
Output value (thousands)	360	6,000	12,500
Output per employee (thousands)	6	50	50
Added value per employee (thousands)	2.8	20	25
Location	M	LT	RT
Electric			
Number of employed	70	300	650
Output value (thousands)	300	6,600	18,400
Output per employee (thousands)	9	22	28
Added value per employee (thousands)	40	12	16
Location	M	LT	RT
Construction			
Number of employed	—	40	50
Output value (thousands)	—	800	13,000
Output per employee (thousands)	—	20	26
Added value per employee (thousands)	—	12	16
Location	—	MT	RT

Table 3–5: Service Institutions and Organizations:
The Normative Parameters for the Local Level of the Development Frame of Reference

Type	Characteristics	Stages of Economic Growth		
		Primary Material Needs	Social Competition	Full Affluency
Primary School	Number of employed	15	30	30
	Added value per employee ($)	2,800	7,000	13,000
	Size of population served	1,500–2,000	3,000–7,000	2,000–3,000
Secondary School	Number of employed	30	45	50
	Added value per employee ($)	3,200	10,000	15,000
	Size of population served	5,000–6,000	8,000–10,000	6,000–8,000
Local Clinic	Number of employed	10	10	5
	Added value per employee ($)	3,200	10,000	15,000
	Size of population served	5,000–6,000	8,000–10,000	5,000
Hospital	Number of employed	170	400	800
	Added value per employee ($)	5,000	12,000	20,000
	Size of population served	150,000	150,000	250,000

Grocery	Number of employed	2	3	20
	Added value per employee ($)	1,800	6,000	2,000
	Size of population served	1,500	1,500	5,000
Community Center	Number of employed	20	15	45
	Added value per employee ($)	2,500	7,000	15,000
	Size of population served	150,000	150,000	250,000
Transport Companies	Number of employed	15	25	35
	Added value per employee ($)	2,500	7,000	13,000
	Size of population served	5,000	10,000	250
Banks	Number of employed	4	5	10
	Added value per employee ($)	3,200	10,000	18,000
	Size of population served	6,000	10,000	50,000
Local Government	Number of employed	20	15	30
	Added value per employee ($)	3,000	7,000	15,000
	Size of population served	8,000	20,000	50,000

core to the periphery. These calculations, while empirically rooted in economic trends, are *projections* for the *future*. In other words, the normative parameters and the optimal mixes I present below are empirically based extrapolations into the future that I regard as indicative of basic patterns in the economic growth process. Undoubtedly, further research may revise the particular values derived. Nevertheless, I believe that the figures given provide the rough order of magnitude for latent patterns of economic growth, which is all that can be expected (see Table 3-6). Though mindful of the limitations of the Frame of Reference, I believe that planners working in the Third World can use it to focus their work by systematically orienting development objectives to conform to the normative parameters.

The Development Frame of Reference succinctly describes the direction of changes that will maximize production capacity and income distribution in order to satisfy the "natural" demands of the population. At first, a developing country must strive to meet the primary material needs of the population, that is, increase food production and domestic consumption. Food production necessarily involves expanding and improving agricultural production structures, though not all agricultural production will result in furthering this goal. For example, in the El-Sisal project in the Dominican Republic,[18] agricultural production increased with no positive effect on economic growth. This apparent anomaly was the result of an expansion in the production of an indigenous staple crop in order to take advantage of favorable exporting market conditions; the crop had by contract to be exported, while the very same crop had to be imported to meet minimal food needs; this bizarre scenario resulted in a negative balance of trade, since importation costs exceeded export revenues.

There are other economic incongruities between subsistence agriculture and current development needs, particularly in the employment structures of traditional farming. By institutionalizing underemployment during slack agricultural seasons, subsistence farming makes inadequate use of its labor resources. But the under-utilization of the human production factor can also be a result of premature and indiscriminate mechanization. Yilmaz Gurer[19] points to three counterproductive aspects of "modernization" (mechanization of agriculture, faulty land reforms, and intensive farming, i.e., the monoculture of cash crops) that directly lead to the underutilization of labor resources at least as much as subsistence agriculture does. Israeli planners have observed similar consequences in misconceived agrarian reform in Haiti,[20] Zambia,[21] and in Kenya.[22]

Modern technology must be used in developing countries to increase the productivity of human labor, not to replace it. While mechanized agriculture may result in higher crop yields, if unemployment and underemployment are thereby increased, the higher yields will benefit the landlords at a social cost for the economy as a whole. Constructive changes in the technology of production that complement, rather than displace labor are what is needed; in Sri Lanka,[23] for example, improved hand tools of simple manufacture greatly increased the productivity of labor in harvesting cotton. Similarly, in Zambia,[24] the introduction of draught animals increased the productivity of labor-intensive agriculture. It is essential that the abundance and potential efficacy of human resources in the developing nations be fully utilized as a prerequisite to accelerated economic growth.

In Sri Lanka,[25] agricultural production evolved from traditional subsistence farming to plantation monoculture, mainly in tea, rubber, and coconut production. While gross production was increased, it failed both to meet the country's food needs and to generate the additional income necessary to purchase food on the world market. Agricultural production must be increased during the initial growth stages in the developing countries. However, it is of equal importance that the change in production structures be in accordance with overall national requirements, in particular in employment opportunities, appropriate technology, and choice of commodities to be produced.

During the present situation in which the majority of developing countries still find themselves, a major goal of development is the transformation of subsistence agriculture, the remnant of the lost Traditional Equilibrium, which is not capable of meeting the food needs of the rapidly increasing population of the developing nations. Farming should be diversified, with an emphasis on staple crops but not a neglect of cash and industrial crops. Agricultural production in the first stage of economic growth, namely primary needs, must aim at producing the basic necessities for an adequate diet on a national scale. Since the needs are so formidable, the aim must be to achieve maximum productivity, which requires the

Table 3–6: Strategic Features of Development According to the Development Frame of Reference

Levels of Function (spatial dimension)	Stages of Economic Growth		
	Primary Material Needs	Social Competition	Full Affluency
National			
Production Capacity GNP per Capita ($)	500–1,500	3,000–5,000	Over 8,000
Structure of Supply and Demand	Demand "natural" supply to catch up	Forced demand spurred by social competition	Affluency spreads in levels of society
Employment Structure	Mostly agricultural, industry spreading to rural towns	Industry leading in all regions	Services take the lead in economy
Regional			
Level of Income and Services	Growth rate of incomes and services faster in regions than in nation	Income and services levels almost equal the nation	Income and services levels of region at least equal to the nation

Occupational Patterns	Urban occupational patterns spread out of metropolitan sphere	Urban occupations spread to medium sized towns	Urban-type occupations at rural areas
Forms of Settlement	Growth of medium sized towns	Growth of regional town	Differences between rural and urban space disappear
Local			
Agriculture	6.6–7.2	21.8–40.0	23.3–46.6
Industry	1.2–5.3	3.3–8.7	5.7–12.7
Services	1.6–1.8	4.6–7.5	8.0–12.5
Size of Local Firms by Number of Employees:			
Agriculture	1.2–1.5	2.0–3.0	1.7–2.5
Industry	1.0–3.5	1.3–15.0	4.3–32.5
Services	1.0–7.0	1.8–10.0	2.0–13.3

* Added value per labor day.

optimal utilization of the factors of production, including labor resources and such yield increasing improvements as fertilizers and crop protection chemicals. Since monoculture, even of requisite staple crops, underutilizes labor resources during the slack seasons, it is not an option at this stage of economic growth. Diversified farming offers the only possible alternative for most developing nations at this stage.

To facilitate the diversification of agriculture, some industrial facilities should be developed in the rural areas, especially those enterprises needed for processing agricultural raw materials and providing some of the imports for the improved farming methods as well as employing labor displaced by farm production. Therefore, urban centers should be established and supported, helping disperse improved services and industry throughout the national space.

According to the Development Frame of Reference, once minimum food needs are met, the society will be ready to undertake the second stage of economic growth, namely the stage of social competition. At this stage, industrial development no longer depends on agriculture, and there is a need for higher services, especially in the field of general and vocational education. More sophisticated agricultural techniques, which are specialized and capital intensive, should also be introduced. The emphasis passes, therefore, to private initiative and competition.

At this point, technological innovations, including automation and computerization of the production process, will enable production to meet and exceed demands for goods and services. Full affluency will then be the final stage of the growth process, preceding the advent of Modern Equilibrium.

INTEGRATED DEVELOPMENT PLANNING

Modern, systematic economic development planning is a product of the twentieth century. As it has evolved, planning deals mainly with physical infrastructure and, to a lesser extent, with economic issues.[1] The problem with this approach, which remains in fashion, is that societies are not limited to things physical (or spatial) and economic, but also have institutional and social dimensions. When mapping a new roadway from a provincial town to an outlying village, for example, the planner must consider all the implications of the project—not just the engineering or economic problems. The project will open new possibilities for the villagers and townspeople—and not all of them will be desirable.

This narrow focus, one I have frequently observed and discussed with planners and officials in country after country, is also reflected in the country profiles* assembled for this book, which reveal that planning, in general, is based on a conventional understanding of development. Not only is it confined to economic and physical factors, but it is dealt with only on the national or macro level. Plans, in these surveyed countries as in others, were usually treated as guidelines rather than as official policy. As a result, they were applied sporadically and inconsistently. Each economic sector was treated separately, with little attention paid to the need for integrating activities. Development authority was vested in agencies

*The profiles, prepared by the Rehovot team, included data relating to the content of plans applied in the sample countries, and examined whether and to what extent planning went beyond the conventional economic and physical aspects.

operating only with national officials, that is, agencies that deal with development projects through the offices of various ministries whose mandates are limited to specific areas such as transportation or industry. This resulted in the participation of multiple agencies, with no single agency taking responsibility for the overall development program.

Another reason planning is often unsuccessful is the frequent failure to effectively carry out plans, even though they are announced amidst much pomp. Many projects are plagued by a lack of continuity between regimes, and development schemes often relate more to the political concerns of particular office-holders than to the authentic needs of the population for whom the schemes are intended. Other causes of failure are inadequate capitalization, insufficient resources, and lack of qualified personnel. Moreover, because they frequently deplete already scarce resources, development projects that suffer from inefficiency ultimately hamper development more than if they had never been undertaken.

The all too frequent lack of systems for evaluating progress also hampers development planning. Since it is impossible to foresee all conditions that will arise, unless a project's progress is reviewed at regular intervals, and plans updated in accordance with the latest findings, there is little hope that the final result will have anything to do with the plans made.[2]

Another problem with current planning methodology is the tendency to treat the target population as passive objects. All too often, planners seem ready to manipulate the populace in the same way they would rivers or mountains. Until such time as the needs, beliefs, and abilities of traditional peoples is taken into account in the development process, development will be unsuccessful.

But perhaps the most glaring failures are caused by a lack of communication. Projects initiated at the local level are usually designed by national planners who have little knowledge of local conditions. In most cases, community development projects were undertaken from national capitals as part of uniform countrywide policies because of the mistaken view that economic growth is a process unaffected by spatial differences between regions and within them. What is more, development activity was found to be initiated and executed by many different agencies, employing methodologies that frequently varied within and between regions; these methodologies tended to be different from and at times inconsistent with, existing activities and projects.

Both my research and my experience have led me to recognize that separate national and local development efforts must be coordinated on an intermediary level. A meeting ground for national and local level officials, set up on a formal basis, is absolutely essential for adequate development because it acts as a lens that focuses on the currently divergent national and local concerns of various authorities.

Fortunately, evidence is accumulating that regional level planning is winning recognition among planners. Lloyd Rodwin, for example, relates that in Turkey, regional development is being given serious consideration despite that republic's tradition of rigid centralism.[3] However, even where regional approaches to development have been attempted in Third World countries, the connection between what is planned for on this level, and the national and local ones, is limited.

INTEGRATED REGIONAL PLANNING

A recent study by the International Labor Organization (ILO) has shown that most national development plans treat the agricultural, industrial, and service sectors as if they were totally independent of one another.[4] More often than not, national development programs are defined in terms of "agricultural" or "industrial" development. On one hand, the Soviet Union has emphasized industrialization in its development program, while China based most of her past development plans on an exclusively agrarian program. The ILO study demonstrated the fallibility of unisectoral development; it argued that intersectoral planning, like interdisciplinary planning, is an essential part of the development effort. Chung-Tong and Ip discuss how this lesson has been painfully realized in China:

It has been reported recently [in China], that the policy of "taking grain as the key link" when implemented, especially during the "Gang of Four" period, actually evolved into a policy of "taking grain as the sole link" (*"yi lianqwei yi"*)—that is, a preoccupation with grain production at the expense of cash crops and sideline production. Priority for grain production was stressed in all communes irrespective of soil suitability. . . . Consequently, in representative areas between 1957 and 1976, grain yields increased by 36 percent, yet production cost rose by 54 percent. . . . Moreover, stagnant productivity remained widespread as production in all private plots was restricted; free market activities were discouraged and income distribution in communes was minimized to increase collective accumulation.[5]

Economic growth cannot take place without a shifting interrelationship between the three sectors. At different stages in the growth process, each of the three sectors in turn predominates in the occupational profile of the society and in the national product. At the earliest stage, agriculture is dominant. For example,

In a country like India where over 70 percent of the people depend on agriculture, agricultural development has to get equal priority [with industry] especially when this 70 percent means 400 million people and when industrial plants, being capital-intensive, have only a limited employment generating capacity.[6]

Eventually, however, development must give rise to industrial and, then, to service sector activities if economic growth is to be sustained. The Chinese have begun a concerted effort to sectorally diversify the economic growth process,[7] which lends credence to the view held by many observers that China will soon enter a new stage in its development.[8]

In addition to the interdisciplinary and intersectoral aspects of planning is the *direction* of development initiative, planning, and implementation. The most common approach is the "top-down" methodology, whereby directives for development activities are issued and enforced by the national government as it deems necessary and appropriate.

"Bottom-up" planning has understandably emerged as a response to top-down methodology. The bottom-up planners believe that the local level alone is the best arbiter of development priorities and that local level activities should be vested in "grass-roots" leadership. In this connection T. R. Lakashmanan writes that:

The widespread reaction against "top-down" planning and the desire for decentralized decision-making to represent local interests has often had the perverse effect of inequitable income distribution. New institutions at the village level, such as the "Gram Sarkar" (village government), have been created in Bangladesh, for instance, for the purpose of encouraging participation of villagers to deal with some of the problems of rural areas and mobilize resources toward self-reliant village societies. However, given the realities of economic and political concentration, the control of these organizations passes largely to rural elites.[9]

While reality has continuously and forcefully demonstrated that designs drawn up in remote national capitals, which takes place under the top-down method, are incapable of appreciating the breadth and depth of local level conditions, the bottom-up approach may fail to take national realities into account. Worse, if relied upon alone, it can perpetuate and exacerbate class and other divisions already existing on the local level. There is a need, as Lakashmanan states, for a "whole set of coherent development planning system components that yield the new integrated concept of development. . . . [In] such a system, *development strategies are not 'top-down' or 'bottom-up' but* hybrid."[10]

China,[11] Indonesia,[12] and India[13] have begun to adopt the hybrid approach to development. Still, further elaboration and clarification are needed to determine the dynamics of a development approach that synthesizes the top-down and bottom-up methodologies. The idea of the development region, central to such a new approach, would deal simultaneously with all three economic sectors in an integrated manner, anticipating the growth of society in terms not only of economic structures but also of its spatial, institutional, and social aspects. The functional regional approach to development integrates priorities and capabilities under a national program.

The development region—that sphere toward which planning should be directed—is a geographical area of varying size, topography, and population; it is the realm of "cross-function," where vertical integration, between macro- and micro-realities, and horizontal integration, in which all sectors are planned for by an interdisciplinary effort, take place.

To a large extent, the region *qua* cross-function is an interpretative designation, assigned to an area by development policy-makers, that results in a certain degree of flexibility in defining a region. Conceivably, what was once a single, identifiable geopolitical region may be broken up and some areas incorporated into neighboring regions of the country for the purpose of easing the development process. Jan Lundqvist describes Tanzania's regional boundaries, which changed due to ecological, economic, spatial, and other factors both before and after that country's independence; working from this experience, he defines a development region as that area where economic, spatial, social, and institutional structures justify planning for a single unit.[14] Logically, then, the development region is a largely uniform area with respect to national resources, historic, linguistic, demographic, and economic composition. All of these factors—and many more—go into the delimitation of development regions, but none alone is capable of defining a specific region. In most cases, regions will be contiguous with a specific terrain, economic base, social affiliation, and language, but homogeneity as such in any of these factors cannot be the only consideration.

The region, shaped by the confluence of economic, spatial, institutional, and social structures, is the framework for which plans are drawn up; it is the "focus of functions" inherent to the development process. The region must not be so large that direct contact between the planning team and the local population is impossible, but it must be large enough to allow for the interplay between the three sectors to be fully operationalized, thereby introducing the multiplier effect and generating maximum employment opportunities.

The shape and size of the region are not fixed and immutable; indeed, they may very well change with economic growth. As economic growth takes place, the gap between the rural and urban areas, between different classes, and between other socioeconomic divisions begins to recede. Consequently, wealth, production capacity, and technological advantage are increasingly diffused throughout rural space, and differences between distinct areas steadily diminish.

The planner must not forget to differentiate between the "rural" and "metropolitan" regions during the early stages of economic growth; the urban and rural spheres at these stages are as different from one another as the developed and developing worlds are today. The differences lessen with the advancement of the development process, although they may remain substantial well into the social competition stage.

To fulfill the development aims described here, a new process, which I call "urban decentralization," must come about. The intersectoral approach to development requires that the needs of all three sectors be met, while at the same time diffusing essential economic structures uniformly throughout urban and rural space. Industry and the services entail functions that are most economically realized in urbanized settings—although the development of the computer may change even this. Yet the urbanization process as it has occurred in the developed nations has proven damaging from the point of view of communities of values. The establishment of regional towns, that is, multipurpose settlements, makes it possible to meet the needs of industry and the services while maintaining rural communities of values (in this respect, the successful establishment of such settlements in Israel[15] and Tanzania[16] may provide useful examples for development planners).

The regional town, a rural center where factories and other industrial facilities are situated, can serve as a marketing and service center capable of handling transportation, communications, and other ancillary functions of those structures. Given its relatively high level of educational and cultural opportunities, it is a semi-urban area that, unlike the village, will attract skilled professionals such as teachers, physicians, engineers, accountants, and others. The rural town also includes educational and cultural institutions that are better than what the surrounding villages could ever afford on their own.

The establishment of the regional town in a rural area demands adequate physical planning. Such planning should include physical infrastructures (roads, railways, water conduits, electricity-generating plants, telephone lines, and similar structures); production facilities (including farm and grazing fields, agricultural holdings, and storage structures); industrial and commercial facilities (stores, warehouses, office buildings, and service institutions); and residential housing (homes, apartment buildings, and other habitations, as well as recreational, educational, and cultural facilities).

Physical planning ought to promote equal accessibility to essential structures for rural and urban areas. Well-equipped hospitals, suitable roadways, electrification, water supplies, warehousing, and other facilities have to be equitably distributed throughout the developing society; children from surrounding villages, for example, should be able to obtain a quality education at the regional town high school, and laborers displaced from the agricultural sector should be absorbed into the industrial and service work force without having to venture to distant cities or to foreign countries.

In the course of development, assuming that the principle of uniform accessibility is achieved, artificial divisions in societal space will gradually break down. The subdivision of societies into local, regional, and national levels has significance only during the growth process. They serve as foci for development activity, but the distinctions between them diminish and finally disappear as society achieves Modern Equilibrium. During development, the division of societal space into villages, towns, and cities has a functional meaning; they are, in terms of socioeconomic structures, different. But the differences eventually wither away during the course of sound development, just as income gaps narrow and services and amenities become accessible to all. People, according to their preferences, may *choose* to live in larger or smaller groups, but functional differences in available resources between different types of settlements will be eliminated.

Spatial planning must also preserve communities of values as far as possible. The construction of modern facilities must also include provisions necessary for the spiritual and cultural needs of traditional community life. A mountain revered by a traditional community as the burial grounds of their ancestors should not be dynamited to facilitate the routing of a new railroad. And while relocation of a population from one area to another is undesirable, at times it must be done, but every attempt should be made to keep communities of values intact when it happens.

GROWTH WITHOUT GEOGRAPHIC MOBILITY

The process of economic growth in the West has, as discussed in Chapter 2, been associated with geographic mobility. Geographic mobility and occupational mobility have gone hand in hand since the first industrial revolution. In the proposed model, I concentrated on finding ways to separate occupational mobility from geographical mobility because including aspects of both social and basic values is so important in development planning. Thus, the model tries to create employment in all three sectors within the region, bringing employment opportunities to the people instead of compelling people to move because of their occupations.

Recent technological developments have made this separation of occupational from geographical mobility a reachable goal. The developments are concentrated in four areas:

Energy. The energy crisis has a direct impact on economic growth because economic growth is firmly linked with an increasing consumption of energy per capita. The vast reservoir of energy from natural sources (oil, coal, wood) has shrunk dramatically, but men have bent their minds and their technology to finding the cheapest and quickest alternative forms of energy. I believe therefore that the crisis *will* be solved and any forecast of developments during the next twenty years should be based on this assumption. Moreover, whatever the future sources of energy, the fact remains that the transportation of energy over large distances at decreasing costs is developing fast.

Transportation. The solution of the energy problem will be accompanied by a long-term solution to the problem of transport and haulage, in terms of both efficiency and of their impact on the quality of life. For example, haulage along movable tracks over hundreds of kilometers is already in operation in various parts of the world, and new haulage methods, such as carriage of metals and raw chemicals in closed carriers under pressure, are in an advanced stage of development. Thus, it may become as easy to transport materials and equipment to the workforce as it now is to transport the workforce to the workplace.

Communications. The most dramatic changes will undoubtedly take place in communications. The radical changes of the past twenty years, particularly the mini-computers, laser beams, and the phenomenal improvements made possible by satellites, all show that communications technology will spark far-reaching changes. The need to congregate in large business centers will be dramatically lessened.

Construction. Major advances have been made in construction, including the use of new building materials that make it possible to suit structures to the special requirements of man and nature.

These changes in the components of the spatial system enlarge the possibilities for future spatial planning, easing the economic and technical pressures that led economic growth along the path of increasing urbanization. Taking these changes into account, I have elaborated the strategies of development planning for each of the three stages of economic growth.

PLANNING AT THE PRIMARY NEEDS STAGE

The intersectoral, integrated regional approach to development that I advocate does not mean that the region is the only functional level on which planning takes place. My proposed Development Frame of Reference can be used to guide the planning methods to be applied not only at any given stage of growth, but also at each specific level of functioning.

Planning on the national level, for example, deals with inter-regional coordination both of population movement and the allocation of national resources. National level planning also directs the economic enterprises that affect the nation as a whole, such as electricity generating power plants, international communications centers, and large chemical and metallurgical industries.

To be successful, integrated regional planning must take into consideration the shifts that take place in the economic requirements at each stage in the development process. An agenda of development priorities has to be set up to ensure that certain sectoral activities are implemented before others. While planning requires coordination between sectors across time, there are specific stages in the growth process where activity in one sector predominates. In the primary needs stage, for example, agriculture must be the main focus of development activity; in the social competition stage, the development of the industrial sector becomes the priority.

Economic growth planning at the primary needs stage should be devoted to the agricultural sector. At this stage, labor, material, and capital resources must be mobilized as effectively as possible, with the role of the government in production and the economy as a whole at the fullest extent possible. Since resources are scarce and inadequate, the thrust of economic activity must be to fulfill fundamental food and housing needs and elementary services. The direction of development initiative is top-down. Micro-level planning at this stage is geared toward transforming the subsistence farm, whose evolution depends on the adoption of yield-increasing methods in order to increase the expansion of production capacity. Since labor consumes even when it is not producing, employment for as many workers as possible, outside of the agriculture, if necessary, is critical.

Subsistence agriculture, which is marked by low labor productivity, is incompatible with development. A typical subsistence farm is small, supports a large family, and leaves a large proportion of the rural labor force unemployed or underemployed during many months of the year. Economic development and modernization of the rural areas require an increase in the productivity of agricultural labor. To achieve this objective, progress must be made on three fronts:

- Overcoming underemployment in agriculture by adopting labor-intensive farming systems.
- Raising production by adopting yield-increasing techniques.
- Creating alternative sources of employment by introducing industry related to agriculture, rural industries, and services.

Each sector of society affects every other sector. Therefore, while development activity at the primary stage demands a heavy emphasis on agriculture, the eventual growth of the other sectors must be planned for at the same time that efforts are being made to modernize the agricultural sector. The transition from subsistence farming to commercial agriculture, for instance, requires a new and relatively complex service network for the marketing of products and the use of new methods and services such as improved seeds, fertilizers, crop protection chemicals, improved implements and equipment, credit and other financial support, along with training and guidance.

The traditional service system can no longer meet the needs of the farmer starting on the road to market-oriented agriculture. But the changes that are needed for that transition will result in a fundamental restructuring of the socioeconomic life of the peasant, so that the planner must not only provide support for such changes but direct the changes in a way that is relevant and appropriate to the particular needs and capabilities of the target population.

A joint Haitian-Israeli planning venture in the terribly impoverished Bas Boen area in Haiti's Valley Cul-de-Sac proved disastrous when social conditions were not taken into account by planners:

Prospect for gain, inflated by the experts' planning of exporting vegetables to an American market, deceived [the peasants] into confident, but utterly unrealistic expectations, which the experts proved incapable of restraining. Many peasants hired farm-hands instead of performing the work themselves. The venture ended in bankruptcy after one season, leaving many peasants additionally burdened with personal debts. . . .[17]

Eventually, a new approach to the Bas Boen project, taking into account the extreme underdevelopment of the people in the area, produced a highly successful development program. The earlier plan had called for cooperative structures and financial schemes that were too sophisticated for the peasants at the time. The approach adopted later allowed the villagers to continue their cultivation of private plots while gradually becoming accustomed to participation in a production cooperative; the plan took the form of a managed training farm on which the peasants worked in the time they could spare from the cultivation of their own plots. They were compensated for their work on the training farm by a share of the profits.

A more gradual socioeconomic change, resulting in sounder development, took place in the Kafubu and Kafulafuta areas in Zambia,[18] where work was begun at the earliest bush-clearing stage. In time, after the planners and peasants working together had cleared the land, the planners provided an opportunity for the peasants to organize themselves into six tiny cooperative societies for the purpose of cultivating 400 acres of maize and raising poultry. Since cooperative attitudes were indigenous to the peasants' culture, they adapted to joint enterprises easily. After some modest successes, production cooperatives were grouped together into a single local union of cooperatives. Eventually, as the fruits of cooperative labors increased, the possibility for establishing a cooperative settlement modeled on the Israeli freeholder rural settlement known as the *moshav ovdim*[19] seemed possible. This, too, was successful and resulted in continuing economic growth in the project area.

These experiences emphasize the lack of uniform solutions that would be applicable to all developing communities. A planner must be imaginative when adapting an appropriate approach to local conditions. For instance, planners working in the Dominican Republic's El-Sisal regional development project[20] recognized that the narrow margin that enabled the peasants in the area to survive made them extremely reluctant to experiment with new crops and techniques, an enterprise requiring a big investment of time and labor that called for neglecting the only means they had of supporting themselves, which meant that they would be worse off if the experiment failed. Accordingly, the planners decided to establish an experimental farm for cultivating the new crops. Local peasants who were more open to innovation than their neighbors were offered the opportunity to work on the experimental farm in return for low but secure wages that would enable them and their families to survive even if the project failed. The experiment was successful, and the peasants working at the demonstration farm were recruited to serve as instructors for the community. The peasants had been shown in the field that it was possible for them to improve their income and thereby change their lives. Eventually, the use of the new crops and techniques spread throughout the region, making possible the implementation of the development project.

Changes in the agricultural sector affect and depend on the industrial sector. As agricultural surpluses are sold and the money used for labor-saving technology, such as a pair of oxen or machinery, new employment opportunities must be found; unless the suddenly unemployed can find work in the rural area they will emigrate to urban areas. That is why I believe that it is critical to begin preparations for an expanded industrial sector as soon as society as a whole can meet its primary needs. The main thrust of industrialization at the middle primary needs stage should be the maximum dispersal of industrial enterprises in the rural areas using technology that can be applied in the agricultural sphere, such as industry that is based on the processing of agricultural products and byproducts. In addition, the diversification of crops—for example, the introduction of a commercial crop such as cotton—

can give rise to local industry for the production of textiles, cottonseed oil, and soap, and also create a previously nonexistent market for perishable products such as vegetables, eggs, milk, and meat.

The infrastructure established for emerging industry should, as far as possible, be as beneficial to agriculture as it is to industry. Roads, water conduits, electrical plants, and other infrastructure and service support systems should be created for all sectors at the same time. Industrial and agricultural development thus give rise to a service sector that will expand as they do. The development planner must be prepared to take into account the sectoral shifts that will occur as development progresses with each stage.*

PLANNING AT THE SOCIAL COMPETITION STAGE

At the stage of social competition, the government should no longer be the major promoter of development change. Instead, nongovernmental initiative should predominate, and a bottom-up approach from the local and regional levels should come to the fore. At this stage, although society is able to meet the primary needs of the population, it will still encounter difficulties. Demand still exceeds production capacity, and some essential goods will remain scarce. Skills and technology remain largely confined to major cities since there has not yet been a substantial diffusion of resources into the outlying areas.

At this stage, government should, when necessary, direct nongovernmental forces toward the industrial sector. For reasons that require much more study and debate, nongovernmental initiative has consistently been associated with the expansion of productions.**

*The country profiles provided a wealth of information about development planning at each stage of growth. These materials have been summarized in tables that show the major planning patterns for each of the stages. See Appendix A.

**This is an analytic statement, and not a normative conclusion. It may be possible for government alone to expand production capacity and structures adequately under proper conditions. However, the facts that emerged from the country profiles collected strongly link private initiative with expanded production.

Whether through tax incentives, subsidization, decree, or otherwise, the purpose of government at this stage of economic growth should therefore be to facilitate the private sector in pioneering industrial production, both in terms of expansion of existing industries and entry into new industrial subsectors.

The gradual accumulation of saved capital in the later primary needs stage accelerates in the social competition stage. Capital is invested in new production technology that increases yield while altering the occupational profile. At this point in the growth process, capital, not labor, is the catalytic factor in the economy because industry, the primary sector emphasized at this stage, is capital-intensive. Agriculture and services follow suit and also adjust to capital-intensive technology.

At the local level, agriculture must undergo another structural transformation. As an outgrowth of an expanding cash market economy, diversification gives way to specialized farming. Goods needed for farm family consumption are no longer raised on each family farm, but are purchased from a commercial outlet. Agricultural yields now exceed those derived under diversified agriculture. An expanding infrastructure expedites the movement of workers and goods while a higher order technology takes over in industry. Synthetic materials begin to overtake agricultural raw materials in the manufacturing of goods.

Government's role in the economic growth process at this stage is mainly in the sphere of regulation, such as antitrust and anti-monopolization laws and statutes against price fixing, to protect the society from economic, social, environmental, or other forms of exploitation that may be initiated by private enterprise. Government intervention is also needed at this stage to divert nongovernment initiative toward the services, so that new and more efficient means of transportation, communication, energy exploitation, financial services, and other support functions are generated.*

PLANNING FOR FULL AFFLUENCY

As societies advance from the social competition stage to the stage of full affluency, labor-intensive production will be largely

*The spatial system thereby created is shown in Appendix A, Table A.2.

replaced by capital-intensive automated and computerized production facilities. At this stage a new kind of technology of production takes over which can be referred to as "know-how intensive"; the production technology may be both labor and capital intensive. Activity in the service sector will predominate over the other two sectors, since decreasing proportions of the labor force are required in agriculture and industry. The diffusion of advanced communication and transportation facilities will bring about "dialogue" between local and national authorities. Accordingly, the intermediate level of the region loses its significance.

As a society approaches full affluency, the priority of development will be reshaping society. It should be fully understood that the production methods will require only workers of high skill and training, with a broad educational base. The white-collar worker will take over from the blue-collar, and the traditional division in employment will gradually and finally disappear. While no country has yet attained full affluency, several countries, for example, Switzerland, Sweden, and Holland, are approaching this stage. The trends I have observed in these countries, as well as other data, make it possible to see the shape of planning for full affluency (see Appendix A, Table A.3).

Current and foreseeable changes in various elements of the spatial environment point to one major conclusion: the possibilities for human control of the immediate environment are expanding. The ever-increasing latitude with which physical planners are now capable of translating ideas into reality will permit the satisfaction of all primary material needs at a heightened level of comfort.

In spite of the Orwellian bogies that are all too often put before mankind as a warning of the dangers of ultramodern technology for society and the individual, the technology of the future is not likely to prove more alienating than our present technology, provided one essential condition is observed: that the welfare of communities of values is preserved.

INTEGRATED DEVELOPMENT PLANNING

What I am proposing—integrated regional planning that will bring about economic development without destroying communities of values—is not an entirely untested theory. On the contrary, several examples are now in place.

The region of Pacosan in Peru offers one example of a compre-hensive integrated regional development plan at work. In 1981, a fifteen-year development plan was drawn up for the region, which embraces three provinces in northwestern Peru—Pascamayo, Contumaza, and San Miguel—by a planning team of the Rehovot Settlement Study Centre that I head.

The total area of the planning region is more than 6,900 square kilometers. The region differs in elevation from sea level to 2,600 meters above sea level, which means that there are major climatic variations. The areas closer to the coast have a constant temperature of 20 to 22 degrees centigrade and a relative humidity of some 80 percent, but a very small amount of rain—no more than 100 millimeters annually. Soil quality is favorable for agriculture in most of the region.

The inland areas (elevation of between 500 meters above sea level up to 2,600 meters) are much colder, with variations in temperature from six to nineteen degrees centigrade according to the season and elevation. Average humidity is the same 80 percent that it is in the coastal area, but annual precipitation varies from 100 millimeters to 400 millimeters annually. The soil in this area is favorable for agriculture only in the valleys: the slopes of the hills can be used only for natural pasturage.

The agriculture in the coastal part of the region includes mainly irrigated rice yielding relatively high crops; livestock (dairy cattle, pigs) and poultry are also raised. In contrast, the agriculture on the highlands is mainly of a subsistence character, the main crops being potatoes, maize, wheat, and barley.

For the most part, industry in the region is not developed; where it is, it is mainly of a low standard, confined in large measure to the initial processing of agricultural products. All industrial plants are located in the coastal area; these include among others a cement factory, asbestos factory, and rice and sugar mills. In the highlands, industry is mainly handicrafts, such as simple weaving. The same difference in development holds for services and infrastructure—the coastal region has far more developed public and private service sectors and infrastructure networks.

The region as a whole is less developed than the nation; for example, the average per capita income (value added) in the region is less than half of the national average. Agriculture in the region employs 57 percent of the labor force, while the national average is

40 percent. However, due to the rather developed agriculture in the coastal area of the region, the average income per employee in this sector is much higher than the national average.*

The main targets of the fifteen-year development plan for the Pacosan region were:

1. Preventing out-migration from the region to the metropolitan areas by providing employment opportunities;
2. Reducing the income gap between the regional and national averages;
3. Reducing the income gap between the various sectors in the region—namely, increasing the average income in agriculture at a higher rate than that of the other two sectors; and
4. Improving the level of public services to the population in the region and creating better accessibility to services.

The plan calls for per capita income (value added) in the region to increase at a rate of 4.4 percent per annum, as compared with about 2.5 percent on the national average, for the last twenty years between 1960 and 1980. The increase in the average income per employee in the agricultural sector in the region should be much higher than that of the other sectors, thus reducing the existing gap between sectors in the region. Employment in services should grow at a much higher rate than the total population growth, increasing the ratio of employees per 1,000 considerably (see Table 4-2).

The plan concentrates services for the population so that services can be provided more efficiently. In the villages proper, very limited services are planned—a kindergarten, a first aid clinic, a grocery. The rural center will provide basic services such as elementary education, health care (including a doctor), small businesses, post, sports. More sophisticated services such as secondary education, central health service (hospital), and banking will be located in the small urban center—subregional centers or the regional center, which is the main town in the region.

The concentration of services and the massive planned industrialization should result in substantial urbanization in the region. The percentage of urban population is expected to rise from 52 percent in 1981 to 66 percent in 1996 (see Table 4-3).

*The main economic and demographic characteristics of the region are compared with the national averages in Table 4-1.

Table 4–1: Population, Employment, and Income in the Pacosan Development Region of Peru

Items	Population	Total	Agriculture	Industry	Service
National Figures					
Total Population (thousands)	17,400				
Labor Force (thousands)		5,480	2,200	1,040	2,240
Percentage of Labor Force in Total Population	100	31.5			
Percentage of Labor Force by Sector		100	40	19	41
Value Added (millions of $)		19,240	1,540	8,660	9,040
Value Added (%)		100	8	45	47
Value Added per Employee ($)		3,510	700	8,325	4,035
Value Added per Capita ($)		1,105			
Regional Figures					
Total Population (thousands)	200				
Percentage of Labor Force in Total Population	100	62.1	35.5	10.4	16.2
Percentage of Labor Force by Sector		100	57.0	17.0	26.0
Value Added (millions of $)		110	49.0	35.0	26.0
Value Added (%)		100	45.0	32.0	23.0
Value Added per Employee ($)		1,770	1,380	3,365	1,604
Value Added per Capita ($)		550			

Table 4-2: Planned Growth in Demographic and Economic Parameters in the Pacosan Region (1981-1996)

Parameter	Absolute Figures (1996)	Average Annual Growth Rate
Population (thousands)	303.1	2.8
Labor Force Total	96.8	3.0
Agriculture	38.9	0.6
Industry	26.0	6.3
Services	31.9	4.6
Total Value Added (millions of $)	318.0	7.3
Agriculture	101.0	5.0
Industry	127.0	8.9
Services	90.0	8.6
Value Added per Employee ($)	3,280.0	4.2
Value Added per Employee in Agriculture ($)	2,590.0	4.3
Value Added per Employee in Industry ($)	4,900.0	2.5
Value Added per Employee in Services ($)	2,815.0	3.8
Value Added per Capita ($)	1,050.0	4.4

Table 4–3: Rate of Urbanization in the Pacosan Development Region

	Total Population		Urban		Rural	
	Absolute (thousands)	%	Absolute (thousands)	%	Absolute (thousands)	%
National Figures (1980)	17,400	100	11,660	67	5,740	33
Regional Figures (1981)	200	100	104	52	96	48
Regional Figures (1996)	303	100	199	66	104	34

Other Examples of Regional Planning. To a large extent, the principles advocated here appear to have been independently applied in China, but there has not been sufficient documentation of the Chinese development programs to warrant including examples from the Chinese experience. However, the approach I am suggesting has been carried out and studied in regional projects in Israel and Holland.

The Lachish region in Israel, for instance, was the locale of a large-scale development program that began in 1955 based on an integrated and regional approach to planning and implementation. The project sought to develop both rural and urban elements in a new settlement scheme that would ensure balanced growth without inducing the out-migration of redundant agricultural labor.

The spatial planning of the region involved three types of settlements: the agricultural village, with an average of eighty agricultural holdings; the rural center, which provides services for every six to eight villages; and the urban center—a regional town—providing more specialized services for the entire region.

Today, there are fifty-six agricultural villages in the region, with 4,500 agricultural holdings compared to some 1,500 holdings in 1955. There are four rural centers, which provide such social services as an elementary school, clinic, general store, cultural center, bank, central garage, and transportation center. Each rural center has about 100 residential units for service workers.

The regional town, Kiriat Gat, was originally planned for a population of 8,000. A generation later, in 1979, the town had a population of 24,000. The services provided by the urban center to the rural periphery include economic production facilities such as agricultural processing plants, a commercial center, sorting and packing plants for agricultural produce, as well as such social services as a central clinic.

Most of the agricultural settlers in the region came from traditional societies in developing countries, mainly in North Africa and West Asia. On average, the first settlers included few skilled workers and professionals. There were five to six children per family. Consequently, teachers, nurses, clerks, and other professionals had to be recruited from among veteran Israelis outside the region.

In the twenty-five years since the development of the region began, a second generation has grown up and founded families of their own. All agricultural land was distributed to families at the outset of the project, and no further land is available for additional farm holdings in the area. Under Israeli law, the land holdings are leased on a long-term basis and may not be divided. When the second generation came of age, only one child per family could inherit the land. The other children, up to 80 percent of the second generation, had to be reabsorbed elsewhere in the regional economy to prevent their migration from their communities.

This scenario was taken into account in the original planning of the region, and the integration of rural and urban elements has provided for occupational mobility without geographical displacement. The surplus labor was reabsorbed into the regional economy because the second generation was trained to gradually replace the skilled workers and professionals introduced from outside the region during the project's initial stages. Indeed, the overall demand for professional workers in the rural service centers has increased. Whereas all of the service employees in the rural service centers came from outside the region in 1957, well over 40 percent of such workers in 1980 were native to the region. Of course, the training of the second generation required the creation of a high quality educational system.

The gradual expansion of industrial facilities also provided employment for the second generation. Each rural center offered full services to eight agricultural villages and partial services for an additional five. In 1957, forty families resided in the service centers; currently, there are ninety families in each center. This increase indicates a much greater capacity to absorb redundant labor from other sectors. Current forecasts suggest that within ten years a majority of the service employees in the region will be native to it; most of the Lachish youth are in institutes of higher learning or in technical training schools in anticipation of assuming service positions in the region.

Kiriat Gat, the regional town, was planned on the assumption that the size of the town would be determined solely by the requirements of the region and that the number of industrial and service workers in the town would be commensurate with the needs of the workers in the rural hinterland. Since the regional project began at a low stage of development, industry in the region was initially confined to the processing of agricultural products (e.g., cotton-ginning machines, sugar refineries, powdered-egg factories);

factories for producing agricultural packing materials, accessories, and tools; and workshops for repairing agricultural equipment.

Over the years the planners realized that nonagricultural industries had to be introduced in order to accelerate the development of the town. The rate of economic growth exceeded that of the earlier plan, therefore, the threshold of urban efficiency had to be elevated. In view of the rapid economic expansion, there was a pressing need to increase the physical structures and spatial scope of the town. Within one generation, 800 native sons and daughters were able to replace the skilled labor force brought in from outside the area at the early stage of the project. Table 4-4 shows that the total population of the regional town doubled in less than twenty years, while the total number of employees in the settlement tripled—and yet full employment remained nearly constant.

Table 4-4: Occupation and Employment in Kiriat Gat, 1962-1980

Data	1962	1980
Total Population of the Town	12,000	24,000
Total Number of Employees in the Town	2,560	9,000
Residents of the town:	2,460	6,800
Residents of regional villages:	—	800
Come from outside the region:	100	1,400
Residents of the Town Working Outside the Region	—	400

Perhaps the most impressive of the demographic data is the fact that only one out of every sixty residents of the region works outside Lachish. The proportion of people retained in the region is therefore extremely high, which has served to preserve the indigenous communities of values in spite of substantial economic growth.

Within the period 1962-78,[21] the total population of the region increased from 26,000 to 45,000. A similar rate of increase in the number of people employed in each sector took place, with the greatest rise taking place in industry, where the number of workers increased by a factor of 3.5 in less than a generation. In 1962, over half of the region's economic output was agricultural. Agricultural production has doubled in the sixteen-year period, industrial output increased tenfold, and service output increased fivefold. The growth of the industrial and service sectors took place so rapidly that workers from outside the region had to be brought in temporarily (see Table 4-5). It is important to remember that private initiative at this stage is the main propellent powering economic growth, and therefore, conditions supportive of social competition should be strengthened. Accordingly, the second stage differs considerably from the first, as will be discussed in detail in later chapters.

A less deliberate planning scheme that nonetheless achieved similar standards of development is that of the Polders in Holland. The spatial organization of the Polder region was generally guided by Christaller's theory of central places.[22] His theory posits that market centers develop in space as the result of the rational behavior of consumers and wholesalers in buying and selling goods and services. According to the theory, the "central place" is the nearby urban center.

Representative of the spatial organization of the Polders are northeastern Polder, which was settled immediately after World War II, and the Polder of eastern Flevoland, settled during the 1960s.[23] The spatial organization of northeastern Polder is on three levels: agricultural holdings, scattered throughout the area rather than in villages; the village, which serves as a primary service center for the holdings and as a residential center for service and agricultural workers; and the regional township, where higher-level services are provided. The distance between the agricultural holding and the nearest service village is not more than five kilometers and the distance to the regional township is not more than fourteen kilometers. There are ten service villages and one regional township in the region. A central town, providing higher-level services than the township, also exists.

The eastern Flevoland Polder began twenty years after the northeastern Polder, and its planning included improvements based on experience gained in the development of the earlier

Table 4-5: Development of the Lachish Region, 1962-1978

Data	1962	1978
Number of Agricultural Villages	57	57
Number of Rural Centers	3	4
Number of Urban Settlements	1	1
Total Population	26,000	45,000
Rural population	14,000	22,000
Urban population	12,000	23,000
Total Rural Population Employed	4,460	7,800
Agriculture	3,700	5,000
Industry (mainly in Kiriat Gat)	60	600
Services	700	2,200
Total Urban Population Employed	2,460	6,900
Agriculture (regional villages)	200	100
Industry	1,200	4,000
Services	1,060	2,800

Total Residents of Lachish Region Employed	6,920	(100.0%)	14,700	(100.0%)
Agriculture	3,900	(56.3%)	5,100	(34.6%)
Industry	1,260	(18.3%)	4,600	(31.2%)
Services	1,760	(25.4%)	5,000	(34.2%)
Product (added value, millions of $)	30	(100.0%)	129	(100.0%)
Agriculture	17	(56.6%)	37	(28.6%)
Industry	5.5	(18.4%)	57*	(44.2%)
Services	7.5	(25.0%)	35	(27.2%)
Product per Employee (added value, $)				
Agriculture	4,360		7,250	
Industry	4,400		9,500	
Services	4,250		7,000	
Average Product per Employee	4,340		8,000	

* In 1978 industry employed workers from outside the region. The total industrial output, therefore, is greater than the product of output per industrial worker and the number of industrial workers.

Polder. Greater emphasis was placed on centralizing and strengthening the service system and on removing service centers from the residential areas. Four levels of spatial structures were created: agricultural holdings scattered throughout the region, as in the case of the northeastern Polder; the village, which is the primary service center, though it can lie as far as fifteen kilometers from a given holding; the regional township, which provides the same relatively high-level services as its counterparts in the other Polders; and the central town, which was planned as the locale for regional government offices and upper-level services, such as specialized hospitals. The central town, which can be as far as thirty to thirty-five kilometers from an individual holding, serves a number of Polders, including but not restricted to the one in which it is situated.

The location of the services for both the northeastern and eastern Flevoland Polders are shown in Table 4-6. The spatial structural organization of the eastern Flevoland Polder is far more efficient than that of the northeastern Polder. In ten years its population was greater than that in the northeastern Polder twenty years after its establishment. Growth had been anticipated, and no less than 18 percent of the region's territory had been set apart for industrialization. Sophisticated spatial planning in these regions resulted, albeit somewhat unintentionally, in an integrated regional space with urban and rural elements in optimal economic relationship to one another. Workers displaced from agriculture were reabsorbed in the industrial workforce within their region, despite the fact that the Polders have a higher birthrate than the rest of the Netherlands and, consequently, have a higher proportional labor pool requiring employment.

As in the case of the Lachish region in Israel, the Polders separated occupational mobility from geographical mobility. Their economy was not only able to retain their own surplus labor, but also absorbed part of the unemployed from external urban areas, including Amsterdam. The integrated development of agricultural holdings and urbanized centers in the Polders has led to a feeling of regional pride and belonging; the farmers and townspeople of the region have come to view themselves as part of a united community with common needs and interests.

The Lachish and Polder projects are regional in nature; they

Table 4-6: Spatial Organization of the Northeastern and East Flevoland Polders

Unit	In Service Village	In Regional Township (B)	In Central Town
Kindergarten and Primary School	XX**		
Secondary or Vocational School		XX	
Higher Education			XX
Religious Facilities	XX		
Local Clinic	XX		
Central Clinic or Hospital		XX	
Specialized Hospital			XX
Entertainment, Culture, Sports	XX	XX	
Grocery Store	XX		
Commercial Center		XX	X*
Manufacturing Services (dairy transportation, sorting, packing)	XX	XX	
Government Offices, Training		XX	X
Agricultural Industry		XX	X
Other Light or Medium Industry		XX	X
Heavy Industry			XX

X*–only in Eastern Flevoland.
XX**–same for both.

display the utility of the region *qua* "cross-function" as a vehicle for development change. But the constructive effects of integrated rural development can also be shown on the local level, particularly in the kibbutz form of rural settlement in Israel.

Members of kibbutz settlement collectives have attained an unparalleled stature in the economic, political, military, cultural, and other spheres of Israeli public life. The kibbutzim were first established in 1909 as communal, ideologically socialist, agrarian settlements. In recent years, because of their highly mechanized farming methods, the kibbutzim found themselves unable to employ increasing numbers of the members in agriculture. In the years 1965-68, the kibbutz experienced a doubling of its agricultural output while encountering a decline of 25 percent in the number of workers/settlers it could employ. Within a short period of time, industry became the dominant sector of the kibbutz economy.

In 1965, a kibbutz founded more than a half a century ago in the Jezreel valley experimented with the introduction of an industrial plant for the manufacturing of irrigation pipes. The increase in industrial activity on the kibbutz provided employment for members who had been displaced by improved agricultural productivity. While the spatial needs of the industrial sector caused a reduction in the areas available to agriculture, the kibbutz chose to modify its exclusively agrarian program in order to stem the out-migration of its members. (Tables 4-7 and 4-8 reflect the evolution of the economic and spatial structures of the veteran kibbutz and a group of seven other kibbutzim that evolved in a similar fashion.)

The results of integrated regional development in the Lachish region, the Dutch Polders, and the industrialized kibbutzim are economic growth coupled with the continuity of communities of values. Similar approaches have begun to be applied in the developing countries as well. For instance, the Kabankalan[24] settlement program launched in the Philippines utilized many of the principles described above. The La Joya project in Peru[25] was also planned according to these principles. It is my fervent belief that the planning methods described here can be fruitfully applied throughout the Third World.

Table 4-7: Development of Population, Production, and Output of a Veteran Israeli Kibbutz from 1954–1978

	1954	1965	1978
Total Population	615	655	767
Total Number Employed			
Agriculture	270	342	349
Industry	104	127	98
	2	2	2
Other (including services)	164	209	144
Value of Agricultural Production ($)	47,500	1,133,660	2,552,650
Value of Industrial Production ($)	5,500	no data	8,035,290
Agricultural Product Added Value ($)	24,167	572,330	1,017,000
Industrial Product Added Value ($)	3,330	27,330	1,300,000
Product per Employed Person			
Agriculture ($)	2,320	4,507	10,380
Industry ($)	1,660	4,555	12,150

Table 4-8: Development of Population, Production, and Output of a
Group of Seven Kibbutzim between 1951 and 1977

	1951	1965	1977
Total Population in the Settlements	3,011	3,198	3,502
Average Population per Settlement	430	457	500
Total Number Employed in Settlements	1,327	1,465	2,126
Agriculture	619	750	533
Industry	38	65	1,142
Other (including services)	670	650	451
Value of Agricultural Production ($)	2,502,000	5,904,000	19,199,000
Value of Industrial Production ($)	147,000	403,600	15,133,000
Agricultural Product Added Value ($)	1,382,300	2,958,000	7,317,300
Industrial Product Added Value ($)	77,000	103,000	6,991,700
Product per Employed Person			
Agriculture ($)	2,230	3,940	13,729
Industry ($)	2,027	1,595	6,122

CHAPTER 5

THE OPTIMAL MIX PRINCIPLE

Those of us who are involved with the nuts and bolts of development implementation have grown accustomed to unexpected conditions and forbidding realities. In the face of underdevelopment, today's planner has few conceptual and analytic tools with which to wage the development struggle. Often, when working on a development project, I have wondered: If there were a formula for planning what would it be able to tell us? How would it help our work in the field? If more resources were available and properly utilized, a country could accelerate its economic growth and thus pass more quickly from one stage to the next, but it is important to remember that the source of the additional resources is a critical factor in development.

Government intervention is necessary in most projects and operations where the objective is economic growth. Indeed, there are certain operations and projects for which the government constitutes the only body that is able to initiate, plan, and implement. Regardless of the manifest or potential strength of private initiative, there are development conditions under which it would be detrimental and futile were it allowed to intervene.

A government has many varied means of intervening and directing the process of economic growth. These may be divided into two principal categories: *financial*, including taxation, customs duties, fixing of interest rates and prices for various commodities, granting of loans and subsidies for production, and, above all, mobilization of capital for investment in new development enterprises; and *organizational*, including marketing directives for production or production limitations, establishment of the structures of various institutions in charge of economic activities, such as the ownership of land, erection of structures in the cities, establishment of credit institutions, information media, institutions for education and vocational guidance, agricultural guidance, and so on. In addition, government can establish economic enterprises under its direct ownership. These may include postal and telephone services, railways, water supply and electricity, or even enterprises of a productive nature, such as factories and agricultural farms.

Establishment of a suitable policy that will enable governments to attain desirable and predetermined objectives requires know-how and proper methodology. All complex processes require advance preparation, that is, "planning." A "plan" may be defined as the sum total of facts and figures indicating the most desirable direction for implementation.

Only the government is capable of initiating and directing countrywide development plans, and even in developed countries one cannot avoid some measure of governmental intervention. Only government can mobilize the extensive capital required for the development of the physical and human infrastructure that forms the basis of any production increases. Further, government is the only body capable of providing education and training to the entire population and of undertaking measures, such as land reform, which clash with vested minority interests. Private initiative is guided by profits and is unable to deploy the vast sums demanded by development.

Private initiative, too, has a significant role to play in the development process. The task of initiating planned growth falls to the state and is of interest mainly to those groups and institutions that motivate the government machine. The implementation of development programs is also to a large extent in the hands of this machine, but because planned development leads to an alignment of social forces, it must embrace all classes of the population and all spheres of activity. Sooner or later the whole society will have to cooperate in one measure or another in the process of development.

It is increasingly clear that economic growth depends on the utilization of private and public forces in a complementary way. The economic system is a product of the interplay between the private sector and government, and the nature of the interplay is in constant flux. The question thus is whether the relationship is arbitrary and random, or whether there is a specific level of interaction between the two sectors which, if attained, will optimize growth at each economic stage. My hypothesis is that there is a predetermined relationship between the sectors that will maximize the growth process—the Optimal Mix Principle.

Underlying this principle is a theoretical assumption: the ratio between government investments and private ones does not depend on the potential of resources but only on the structure of their deployment, according to the specific stage and level at which they operate. This accounts for the existence of rich nations in areas poor in resources and poor nations in areas rich in resources. In order to examine this principle, two preliminary conditions must be fulfilled. First, one must clearly define the possible situations in the process of economic growth; the Frame of Reference does exactly that. Second, we should be able to determine and to define development projects and to measure the relative contributions of government versus private concerns to total investment. For that purpose we should review the principal lines of thought regarding this problem. If development planners accept these assumptions, the principle as formulated can be used in planning strategies for development.

THE CONCEPT OF THE OPTIMAL MIX

Accepting the Optimal Mix Principle as a given, means accepting that there *is* a ratio between government and private forces that maximizes economic growth, but that this ratio changes for different development situations as defined by temporal and spatial dimensions. If patterns correlating the proportion of government investments to private ones can be discovered, then growth can be facilitated by shaping investments in accordance with the optimal mix.

At my behest, the Rehovot team examined the patterns characterizing the investment mixes for each stage in the growth process in an attempt to confirm this hypothesis. A cross-section analysis was made of all the data collected in the country profiles in an effort to discover any patterns. Additionally, the team performed a time-series analysis for four countries (the United Kingdom, France,

Greece, and Israel) for which they were able to obtain reliable information about the development process.

The breakdown of total investments into government and private shares is available only for recent periods, since most countries began keeping national accounts only after World War II. The cross-section analysis was carried out on the basis of two sets of data:

- Data culled from the United Nations National Accounts tables. These data include information for twenty-four mainly developed nations for which enough data are available to compute an average investment mix (the ratio of government to total investments) for the period from 1960 to 1975. The sets of years considered for these nations varied from four to eleven years within the 1960-73 period.
- Data from the World Bank. These data were primarily for developing countries whose economies have been studied in detail by the Bank. The investment mix for these countries was defined as the ratio of the capital account of the government budget to the total gross investment of the country.

For both sets of data, structural differences between countries were taken into account by factoring into the calculations regressions in the size of the population, per capita GNP in U.S. dollars, and the average population growth rate for the 1965-73 period by using the accepted statistical regressions method.[1]

The computations for the cross-section analysis of the developed countries (see Appendix B for a detailed presentation of the analysis) suggest that a relationship does exist between the growth rate and the mix of government and private investment and that the relationship does not seem to be a static one. At the early stages of development, government activity seems more effective in advancing economic growth. However, at the middle and higher stages of development, there seems to be an inverse relationship between economic growth and government intervention. This would seem to imply that a decreasing amount of government involvement in the economy and, consequently, an increase in the amount of private investment furthers the growth process.

I am not claiming that the statistics used are characteristic of the economic growth process of all nations. What I do say is that the analysis revealed certain trends, even though the particular values derived might have a considerable margin of error. The general patterns uncovered indicate that there does indeed exist a relationship between government investment in development and economic growth, and that this relationship is not linear. Specifically, there are indications that a certain "upper limit" to government intervention exists and that when this threshold level is exceeded, economic growth declines.

The national time-series analysis on which these conclusions are based has an advantage over cross-section analysis because it eliminates the problems of structural differences between national economies. In time-series analysis, one probes the economic performance of a country relative to itself for different years, while in cross-section analysis one looks at the economic performance of one country in comparison to that of others for the same years. But the choice of a times-series analysis meant relying on a small group of nations for which adequate data could be obtained. The data pool is not statistically representative of all countries for all stages of the development process. It does, however, reveal patterns exhibited by the countries studied—for which minimum data existed.

In preparing the time-series analyses of the four countries under study, it was essential to keep in mind the fact that changes in technology and in production structures take place with the passage of time within the same economic system, and that these changes may operate with some lag between the time they were instituted and the time their effects are noticeable. Also, for the nations studied, there were differences in time periods.

The national time-series analyses were made for the following countries and years: the United Kingdom (1959-77), France (1959-78), Greece (1949-77), and Israel (1962-77). For the United Kingdom, regardless of the way in which the proportion of government to private investments was computed, there was no clear pattern concerning such ratios and the GNP per capita growth indicator. For France, there was a significant negative correlation between government involvement and economic growth; the threshold level appeared to be between 13 and 18 percent of government investments relative to total investments. When government investments exceeded this level, declining growth was noted. For Israel, there appeared to be a direct and positive relationship between economic growth and government investment in the early stages of the economic growth process. When the proportion of government investments in Israel went above 37 percent of total investments, declining growth rates were observed. Greece was similar to Israel in this respect (though the particular ratios of government to total investments was 28 percent for Greece compared to Israel's 37 percent). When government investments rose above 28 percent in Greece, a negative effect on economic growth was noted.

The differences in the results of the cross-section and time-series analyses may be caused by the limits of the statistical information used. In addition, it is important to keep in mind that when the ratio of government to private investments was high, negative growth rates (for France) or no pattern at all (for the United Kingdom) were noted. This would suggest a negative relationship between government investment and economic growth in these *developed* nations. On the other hand, for Israel and Greece, during the early stages of their economic growth, that is, when both countries could be considered to be developing ones, a positive relationship existed between government involvement and economic growth. These trends began to reverse themselves when certain levels of economic growth were attained, representing the passage of these countries out of underdevelopment. That is, after these countries passed into the middle stages of growth, there was a correlation between growth and government involvement comparable to that calculated for France. The different peak values for Israel and Greece (37 percent for Israel; 28 percent for Greece) can be attributed to different economic structures existing in each country and to different socioeconomic priorities.

In taking a close and hard look at the data used and the cases referred to, a number of problems are apparent: the data pool was too small, especially with respect to the time-series analysis; the "developing" countries used in the time-series analysis, Israel and Greece, cannot be considered "typical" developing countries; different time periods were used for different countries; and an ad hoc way of dealing with structural differences between the countries, particularly those studied in the cross-section analysis, raises questions about the numerical precision of the conclusions reached, though not the patterns they indicate.

Even though the data cannot be used to prove conclusively that the investment mix and economic growth are linked, assuming hypothetically that there is a connection between the investment mix and economic growth and using indirect statistical methods, I made a series of projections concerning the order of magnitude for the various optimal mixes at various growth stages. It must be stressed again that this model is not based on statistically representative data reflecting conditions in all development areas in the past, but that does not prevent the creation of a model that suggests the general directions future development should take.

THE TRENDS IN INVESTMENT MIXES

The economic system, as already mentioned, cannot be defined solely in terms of national averages; the relationship between the government/private investment ratio and economic growth on the regional level also has to be analyzed. For this purpose, the region is defined as all of the rural national space, that is, all national space excluding the metropolitan space. The data computed for anything approximating the functional development region as defined here is limited; only France, Holland, and Israel provide regional statistical data in their yearly national data, and then only for fairly recent periods. Indirect methods of analysis therefore had to be used to derive the order of magnitude for the relationship between the public to private investment ratio and economic growth. Figures for various socioeconomic indicators on the local level, the level of the individual production unit, were used. These indicators were derived by using average models of each representative production unit, as described in the questionnaire, such as a farm holding, distinct industrial factories, and various specific service units, for example, a primary school, a field clinic, and a hospital. The values derived were then compounded by the differences in the order of magnitude between the various characteristic elements of the society on the local and regional levels according to the Development Frame of Reference.

To gauge the accuracy of these figures, they were compared to the statistics for France, where metropolitan as well as national averages had been calculated. This allowed a more direct determination of regional data (by deducing the metropolitan average from the national average). The French have kept data for the general gross investment, both public and private, for every major branch in each sector, on the national level. Data concerning employment in these branches were also available for the Paris metropolitan area and for France as a whole. The amount of total investments per employee at the national level for each branch was known, and the assumption was made that the ratios for investments per employee were the same in the Paris region. Knowing the total employment per branch in the Paris region allowed for a comparison of the Paris region and France as a whole.

A similar, though somewhat different, set of calculations was made for South Korea. Data for Bassan, the country's second largest city, was used. In this specific case public investments for both the central and local governments were compared with data concerning private investments in that city (see Table 5-1). Data concerning the shares of the private and public sectors in the total investments of the whole country were obtained from the United Nations National Accounts.[2] It appears that for the Bassan metropolitan area from 1960-73, the government share of the investment mix was 26 percent. It therefore follows that the regional mix was considerably lower than the national mix. This implies that the investment mix for the metropolitan area of Bassan must have been considerably higher than it was for the nonmetropolitan areas.

When a similar calculation was made for the United Kingdom, defining the London region as the average metropolitan region in England and comparing it to the mix for the whole country, a tangible difference between the national and regional mixes was found. These indirect procedures provided general estimates of the relative shares of government and private investments in development projects at the regional level (the details can be found in Appendix B).

ANALYZING THE TRENDS

At the primary material needs stage, the government's share of total investments for development projects on the national level was between 18 and 30 percent, while figures for the regional level were between 11 and 19 percent. During the social competition stage, the national and regional values were 15 to 25 percent and 14 to 20 percent, respectively. At the full affluency stage, the figures are, respectively, 12 to 19 percent and 11 to 20 percent.

Table 5-1: Percentage of Investments for South Korea Made by the Local and Central Authorities Contrasted with the Average Public Investments in the Bassan Metropolitan Area

Year	1976	1975	1974	1973	1972	1971	1970
Public Sector Percentage of Investment (all South Korea)	11.4	11.9	21.7	16.9	18.4	18.4	14.0

Yearly Average for this Period in Metropolitan Bassan = 26%

These trends reveal that the government's investments at the national level are higher in the early stages of economic growth and gradually decrease. While these trends were not observed in the developed countries during the corresponding growth stages, today's developing nations, owing to changes in the size of their populations and innovations in technology, must act to implement such change. Therefore, as the country ascends the ladder of economic growth, the difference in the metropolitan and non-metropolitan investment mix decreases. It is significant that in all developing countries the strategy employed is to concentrate government investments in the metropolitan area while the rest of the country receives only an inconsequential amount of government investment. It is important to realize that economic growth will be dependent on *increasing* investment in the *nonmetropolitan* areas.

To establish a general rule that could indicate the optimal mix for any development project, the analyst must examine the trends for the local level, where projects are classified according to their sector. The computations for each of the units of production dealt with direct investments in the production set-up as well as investments in infrastructures directly connected to each unit of production, but not with the regional or national infrastructural network. In addition, the infrastructures connected with either the process of production or with the housing of the people engaged in each production unit were analyzed.

The unit of agricultural production at the local level is the family farm or the individual farm holding. Included in the operation of such units are investments in the infrastructures, such as land preparation and irrigation systems. The mix was examined at the four levels of growth designated by the Development Frame of Reference. Calculation of the mix was based on the profiles of the nine countries, representing a range of development stages. Time-series analyses were used for some of the countries that had passed from one stage of development to another. For this purpose, the questionnaires for the profiles had requested data for a number of periods—two to four—and thus showed some countries in both developing and developed stages.

When the questionnaires were analyzed, it became possible to compute the ratio of public investment to total general investments for different stages of farm development. When responses to the relevant indicators were not available, a mix was estimated based on information from the literature or indirectly computed by extrapolation. In the literature concerning the financing of growth in the agricultural sector, the share of government participation in the farm itself was examined. Certain development projects in which government investment was high were not analyzed; these projects were considered to be nonrepresentative for most agricultural farms. For example, government investments in the Gal-Oya and Ude Walawe[3] projects of Sri Lanka were considerable and, at times, amounted to about one-third of the total investments required. These investments were, however, limited to only a small percentage of the agricultural farms (see Table 5-2).

Table 5–2: The Rate of Public (Government) Investment in the Total Investments for the Individual Agricultural Farm

Stage of Societal Growth	Percentage of Government Investment of Total Investment
Traditional Stage	10–15
Primary Material Needs Stage	24–40
Social Competition Stage	7–15
Full Affluency Stage	0–5

The industrial sector is even more difficult to analyze, given that figures relating to government investments in typical local-level industrial enterprises have been either nonexistent, or inconsistent from one country profile to another. National-level data were derived from the United Nations' studies and the World Tables of the World Bank.* In the questionnaire, industry was classified in terms of six categories: food and beverages; textiles and clothing; metal work of all kinds; chemical and petrochemical industries; electric and electronic industries; and building industries.

*The World Bank projects served as our data source. However, the share of government investment as calculated on the basis of these projects might be skewed upward, since it is possible that government financing was larger in these specific projects.

In order to see whether the project averages derived from the questionnaire were realistic, they were compared to data from development plans of the same countries as cited in the United Nations' publication entitled "Summaries of Industrial Development Plans."[4] The differences between the results were not significant, except for Kenya, where the public share in industrial development is very small in comparison to the average in the World Bank projects. Since the UN statistics cover earlier years than do those of the World Bank projects, countries could have seen an increase in the government share of investments later on. However, apart from Kenya, the differences are not significant. For comparative purposes, it should be noted that public funds may be channeled by governments through their national banks. Such funds are also included in the public sphere.

The share of public funds in the total investment in lower-income countries such as Pakistan and Zambia is higher than in the other four countries. The share in financing manufacturing in the lower-income countries is, in contrast, relatively lower than that of the second group (see Table 5-3).

The investment mix in the service sector was also analyzed. Service units at the local level are individual enterprises or institutions such as schools, clinics, hospitals, banks, commercial shops and markets, and transportation facilities. These services are divided into four separate groups: *economic services*, including a transportation company, bank, marketing enterprise, and a sorting and packing plant; *social services*, such as a clinic, school, cultural institution, relief organization, and community center; *commercial services*, including shops and wholesale markets; and *administrative services*, such as the offices of the local authority or the local branch of government ministries.

Medical services in the United Kingdom provides an example of the manner in which the mix was evaluated. An examination of the structure of the British national health services,[5] which were established in 1948 and subsequently updated, provided details about the methods of health-care delivery and services, the family doctor system, hospitalization, public health services, and the sources of financing for the health services. In this case, the main investment source was, of course, public. The rate of public investment in this system was critical to its continuation. The

Table 5-3: Investments in Manufacturing by the Public and Private Sectors for the Traditional Stage and Primary Material Needs Stage (by percent) *

Stages	United Nations		World Bank	
	Public	Private	Public	Private
Traditional Stage **	21	79	28	72
Primary Material Stage ***	31	70	30	70

* For the purpose of comparing these countries, the average income of the UN plans for the year cited was multiplied by the 1975 price index.

** Pakistan, Kenya, Tanzania, Nigeria, and Zambia.

*** Turkey, South Korea, Costa Rica, and Mexico.

United Kingdom also displayed a high rate of public financing of educational services, although not as in the health services.

Using analyses such as these allowed for an estimate of the investment mix as deduced at various stages of growth and correlated with several types of services (see Table 5-4).

THE OPTIMAL MIX PRINCIPLE

The trends that I think can be seen in the relationship between economic growth and the way that investments are structured in the countries for which there was some available data have not been much discussed in the literature. The focus of discussions of the link between investments and economic growth generally is on overall investments in the economy; for example, Zisner notes that "in conditions of steady economic growth the average rate of savings per capita is commensurate with the average growth of income per capita. This growth is connected with the rate of economic growth."[6] He found that this pattern is neither determined nor influenced by the importation of capital from abroad.

While this does not preclude the existence of a relationship between economic growth and capital importation, it is important to note that research has indicated that the rate of economic growth of any country is not dependent on capital from abroad but principally—and perhaps solely—on the correct use of economic resources already at the country's disposal. Development planning must be based on the fact that assistance from abroad can, at best, aid economic growth: it cannot replace the optimal deployment of existing and potential indigenous resources.

Economic growth at the earliest stages in developing countries is dependent on the full utilization of labor resources—not on capital. Even if the amount of imported capital is relatively high, it does not compensate for the marginal and often destabilizing effect it can have on a developing society. It is therefore critically important to recognize that economic assistance from outside, whatever its magnitude, cannot replace, in the growth process, economic restructuring. It is the realignment of economic structures, not increases in resources, that determine economic growth levels and rates.

Table 5-4: Investment Mixes for Four Classes of Services Correlated by Development Stage

Type of Service	Traditional Stage	Primary Material Needs Stage	Social Competition Stage	Full Affluency Stage
Social Services (e.g., education, health)	90–100	90–100	70–80	60
Economic Services (e.g., credit, marketing)	70–80	70–80	40–50	60–65
Commercial Services (of all types)		—very low in all stages—		
Administrative Services (mainly governmental)	—very high in all stages, approximately 100%—			

Analyses of the link between economic growth and investment mixes as such are exceedingly rare. Two studies concerning Japan, though, are illuminating. The first, conducted by Nosse in 1973,[7] showed that the share of investments in the total cost of production in Japan gradually increased with economic growth. In general, the government's share of investment was relatively high during the first stages of economic growth and receded as economic growth advanced. A second study of Japan carried out by Okawa and Rosovsky in 1973[8] showed that the relationship between public and private investments was that of leader and follower: when private initiative leads, the government's task is to make up what is lacking, but when private initiative fails to fulfill the function of leader in the economy, the government should enter the picture and assume a leadership role. An analysis of the history of Japan's economic growth between 1897 and 1962 reveals that private initiative and government intervention exchanged roles as leader and follower with regard to investments and development in the early stages of development.

The foregoing suggests that a relationship does in fact exist between the level of government investment and the rate of economic growth. Up to a certain point, government investments seem to help define and establish the rate of economic growth; however, beyond this limit, its influence recedes, although it can decrease or even stop the rate of growth. The threshold level changes with economic growth; it is high at low levels of economic growth, while receding commensurately with a rise in the level of economic growth. The values arrived at in my studies suggest a range between 25 to 27 percent for the first stage of development, and beneath 15 to 19 percent for the later stages.

In general, then, economic growth is dependent on the proportion of resources—both public and private—allocated for development projects, and there is likely to be a fixed ratio between government investment and private initiative that optimizes the development of projects regardless of the quantity of resources deployed.

I want to emphasize that the rates of the optimal mix for the country as a whole—as expressed by national averages—are not dependent on the quantity or nature of the resources available to the society. The amount of natural resources determines the rate of economic growth, and it accounts for the ability of a rich country to pass more speedily from one stage to another along the scale of economic growth. But the quantities of resources do not influence the optimal mix of investments for a particular development situation. A high rate of population growth tends to impede the country's capacity for ascending the ladder of economic growth. However, it appears that population size does not change the ratio of the optimal mix for investments at any given stage of growth.

Adequate government incentives are necessary for the full participation of private initiative in all parts of the country. Consequently, the optimal mix of investments at each of the three functional levels—the national, regional, and local—will be different. As economic growth occurs, differences between metropolitan areas and other regions of the country recede and eventually disappear. When economic activity is characterized by integration between sectors throughout the national economic system, the optimal mix for the three levels is more or less equal. Due to a lack of investment mobility, development, instead of deriving strength from the center for a diffusion of activities into the surrounding regions, takes the opposite direction; resources move from the periphery to the center, that is, to the metropolitan area(s) of the country.

Unfortunately, governments, impressed with the strength of this movement from the periphery to the center, have tended to allocate the majority of their investments to the central metropolitan region on the assumption that this will produce growth in the economic system as a whole. Accordingly, present-day investment policy in poor countries is exactly the opposite of that dictated by the Optimal Mix Principle, and has brought about an overemphasis on industrial activity concentrated in urban areas.

Each of the growth stages requires a different mix. In the primary material needs stage, at a time when capital accumulation is miniscule, the main stress is on the full and effective employment of the labor force. The social competition stage is marked by the need for a complete balance between labor and capital, especially since sectoral shifts demand that agriculture decrease its use of labor resources to free labor to participate in industry. At full affluency, technological know-how, particularly that which will come in the wake of the Second Industrial Revolution, will result in the increasing transfer of human labor from material to more cultural and spiritual production; in other words, from work in the classic sense to leisure in the modern sense.

Tables 5-5, 5-6, 5-7, and 5-8 correlate the various values computed for the optimal mixes for different combinations of stages of growth, levels of functioning, and sectoral emphasis. Again, they are not intended as a representation of the development process in the past; they merely reflect the likely order of magnitude of the optimal mixes once more conclusive statistical analysis can be made. Nonetheless, I believe that these figures can be useful guidelines for those directing development activity.

Table 5–5: The Optimal Mix for the National Level at Each Stage of Growth for the Countries under Consideration (by percent)

Stage Source	Primary Material Needs	Social Competition	Full Affluency
Public	30	20	15
Private	70	80	85

While the structure of the optimal mix indicates a steadily decreasing level of government investments, two diverse processes take place simultaneously: government intervention on the national level increases from about a tenth in the first stage to a quarter in the third stage. On the other hand, government participation on the local level diminishes at a greater rate than its increase on the national level, from about a third in the first stage to a negligible amount in the third stage. A similar process occurs at the regional level. The distribution of government investments among the three levels is of primary importance. In the first stage, 20 percent of the government investment should be directed to the regional and local levels combined, with the main stress on the regional level. In the second stage, the distribution of investments between the three levels should be more or less equal, and in the third stage the emphasis of government investments passes to the national and regional levels.

Table 5–6: The Breakdown of the Optimal Mix for the Countries under Consideration at Each Stage of Growth by Level of Societal Functioning (by percent) *

Stage	Primary Material Needs		Social Competition		Full Affluency	
	Public	Private	Public	Private	Public	Private
National	10	50	35	30	40	20
Regional	50	10	35	20	40	20
Local	40	40	30	50	20	60

* These figures indicate the disaggregation of government and private investments for the three levels of societal functioning expressed by percentage.

Table 5-7: The Breakdown of Public and Private Investments (by percent)

Level	Primary Material Needs			Social Competition			Full Affluency		
	Public	Private		Public	Private		Public	Private	
National	8	92	= 100%	23	77	= 100%	26	74	= 100%
Regional	68	32	= 100%	30	70	= 100%	26	74	= 100%
Local	30	70	= 100%	13	87	= 100%	5	95	= 100%

Table 5–8: Projections for the Allocation of Public and Private Resources for the Three Stages and Three Levels of Functioning (by percent)

Level	Primary Material Needs		Social Competition		Full Affluency	
	Public	Private	Public	Private	Public	Private
National	3	35	7	24	6	17
Regional	15	7	7	16	6	17
Local	12	28	6	40	3	51
Subtotal	30 +	70	20 +	80	15 +	85
Total	100		100		100	

The full practical significance of the optimal mix, as systemized by the Development Frame of Reference, cannot be regarded as complete without an analysis of local-level activity (see Table 5-9). The development of economic and social services on the regional and local levels during the initial stages of growth clearly needs to be given preference if the applications of relatively large investments in the agricultural sector are to be helpful, for the full cooperation of rural populations is a necessary component for the development of the inherent resources of a region or nation. In addition, the government must assume an active and supporting role for industry at the local and regional levels.

The systematic application of the optimal mix of investments as scheduled by the Development Frame of Reference can become a powerful instrument for effecting economic growth, particularly during its earliest stages. Greater specificity and empirical analysis must be undertaken before the concept of optimal mixes can be practically applied. In the interim, I believe that the patterns that I discerned in my analysis can be usefully employed in development work.

Table 5-9: The Optimal Mix of Investments at the Local Level *

Stage Economic Sectors and Subsectors	Primary Material Needs		Social Competition		Full Affluency	
	Public	Private	Public	Private	Public	Private
Agriculture	35	65	15	85	5	95
Industry	40	60	20	80	10	90
Economic Services	70	30	50	50	40	60
Social Services	100	—	80	20	60	40
Commercial Services	10	90	—	100	—	100
Administrative Services	100	—	100	—	90	10

* Construction investments, building, and infrastructures were included in each sector according to their particular requirements.

CHAPTER 6

THE INSTITUTIONAL STRUCTURE OF DEVELOPMENT

Development planning, particularly when based on the concept of the development region, requires decentralization. The effectiveness of a development program is often directly related to the degree of mass participation and cooperation it enjoys. In discussing India's Community Development Program, Anand Sarup noted:

[development cannot] succeed unless there is a high degree of rapport between the people and the program administration. This rapport can be built up only when those engaged in community development go to the people in order to *participate* in the process of identifying needs, finding solutions and developing logically acceptable methods of dealing with problems.[1]

Yugoslavia provides what may well be the most far-reaching example of decentralization in the world. As a federation of administratively autonomous republics, regions, and districts that correspond largely to ethnic divisions in the society, Yugoslavia bases its economic policy on the doctrine of self-administration;[2] the result is a "dialogue" between federal, regional, and local authorities—and for these purposes "authorities" has been extended to include, in addition to governmental bodies, such groups as labor councils, consumer cooperatives, and farmers associations. While Yugoslavia's system of decentralization is far from flawless, it does constitute a precedent for successful development through cooperation on many levels and through broad participation in the decisionmaking process. This is illustrated by the proliferation over the years of participatory institutions through which the Yugoslav citizen can exercise influence on economic and settlement matters. For example, the Yugoslavian government notes that the number of workers' councils ("radnicki saveti") leapt from 4,646 in 1952 to 22,151 in 1976. All told, there are over 80,000 institutional groupings relating to various aspects of economic life in Yugoslavia, including "basic organizations of associated labor," "working communities," and "self-managing communities of interest" (there are 3,427 in this category, which includes communes).[3]

Other states have also introduced various degrees of decentralization in development. Among the most notable is China,[4] particularly with respect to the *xian* administrative unit, which is, in essence, a functional development region. It is interesting to note that this trend is not solely limited to developing countries but is now also being adopted in such developed countries as France and Britain, particularly on economic and ecological issues. In recent years, Spain has fully adopted this approach and has created regions that have far-reaching statutory and administrative independence. Unfortunately, as shall become clear, good intentions and even far-reaching decisiveness are not enough without the know-how to implement development.

Of course, decentralization is difficult to achieve. Given the way that most governments are structured—from the top down—decisions are made by the leaders in the capital for the nation as a whole. And what is best for the nation as a whole is all too often defined by those seeking to maintain power as that result which is the most visible and the most quickly achieved. Since development planning for specific regions draws excessively on national resources and does not achieve visible national results for a long time, it often has little political appeal. In addition, there are times when circumstances make it difficult for the government in power (no matter how much it may want to promote the long-term good of the nation as a whole) to foster development change.

Although it is impossible for development to remain entirely aloof from politics, the mutual goal of planner and politician should be as much separation of politics and political power and economic development planning as possible. For example, when political difficulties in a developing country do not seem likely to be solved quickly, development institutions can be separated from politics; in the Philippines in the 1950s, public nongovernmental development authorities (the Philippine Rural Reconstruction Movement and the Philippine Rural Community Improvement Society)[5] were established in the midst of political turmoil that was wracking the nation. Unfortunately, this line was not adhered to, and subsequent governments in that country regressed to centralized machinery. As a result, the promising plans formulated by these agencies were not brought to fruition.

As we shall see, however, even when national political difficulties are overcome and a more decentralized approach is accepted as the only way to improve life for everyone in the society in the long run, the work has just begun.

THE ORGANIZATIONAL PROBLEMS

The problems that must be overcome before development planning can succeed are mainly found within the government bureaucracies. They too are centralized institutions, and they are engaged in holding onto and, when possible, increasing their power. The result is a tendency, particularly among government agencies, to plan and execute regional and local activities in isolation from other agencies and from the people of the region and in accordance with the directives from above; what follows is waste, duplication, and inevitably, failure.[6]

Albert Waterson succinctly describes the current problems with institutional structures in development:

Few countries can cope with the administrative problems which development planning brings. These problems are so complex that in most less developed countries the limitation in implementing plans is not financial resources, but administrative capacity. . . .[7]

Development planning, particularly decentralized development planning, will require changes in the institutional structures responsible for development. These changes should bring about a new institutional infrastructure capable of handling every aspect of development on every level. These institutions must cover the nation, reaching into each region of the country, and the institutions must communicate—each level within a given institution, each institution with every other, and always with the people who will be involved in the development process.

Furthermore, since each of the stages of development has distinct tactical aims, and the means needed to attain these aims vary, the institutional structures must be planned in such a way that they will be able to accommodate the changing needs of development as strides are made; for these purposes, the institutions must include channels of communication between development officials, the people, and private entities involved in infrastructural change.

The largest institutional structures are governmental agencies. There are, of course, also nongovernmental institutions involved in the infrastructures of society. These can be broken down into private and public organizations. The private groups include companies, corporations, estate farms, warehouses, and private purveyors of services involved in economic pursuits. Among the public nongovernmental groups involved in the infrastructure of developing societies are peasant associations, marketing boards, trade unions, consumer cooperatives, communes, and artisans organizations. *All* of these groups must be recruited and actively involved in development.

Unfortunately, efforts aimed at coordinating the efforts of so many diverse groups often—and unnecessarily—result in burgeoning bureaucracies. The resources that are expended in creating and running the bureaucracies represent just the kind of wastage that good planning should prevent. The emphasis, whenever possible, should be on improving and expanding lines of communications, streamlining and realigning procedures, and coordinating related activities rather than on building new, discrete institutions.

The government agencies that function as development authorities must, thus, fulfill three roles in the growth process. The first involves meeting the government's share of investments according to the Optimal Mix Principle for each stage as defined by the Development Frame of Reference. The second role entails assisting the private sector in playing its part in the economy effectively. The third role is the formulation of plans for development projects at each stage of functioning and at each stage of growth.

The second role can be best illustrated by an example:

Modern agriculture should be based on family farms owned and cultivated by enterprising farmers who can handle the ever-changing demands of new technologies, marketing procedures, and organizational structures. The main task of developing countries is therefore to transform their peasants into enterprising farmers—a lengthy process, laden with obstacles, mostly social and political in nature.

In the early stages of its economic growth, Israel discovered that by using large managed farms as temporary agents for rural transformation, many of these obstacles could be overcome. This method requires planning for areas designated for development in such a way that they will be able to satisfy the future needs of the farmers, such as main roads, canals, and peripheral infrastructure; but all agricultural resources—land, water, implements, and so forth—are entrusted to private individuals or to large companies, to be handled much as "managed farms for development" are. Candidate farmers reside in the villages and are employed by the managed farms as laborers for a period of adaptation and training. Following this period, the managed farms are subdivided and handed over to their new owners, who have become trained farmers. The duration of the training period varies according to social and ecological factors, and could last from ten to twenty years.

The managing agencies of the managed farms themselves were also responsible for the development of economic services, that is, marketing facilities, purchasing centers, and experimental plots, as well as the basic infrastructure of the region. Moreover, several managed farms would join forces to establish industries for the processing and handling of agricultural production and raw materials. As the training period came to an end, industrial enterprises usually remained the property of the managed farms, either in full or in part.

Private enterprise was thus utilized for three purposes:

- To transform peasants into enterprising farmers, the most dependable social strata in rural areas.

- To utilize agricultural resources through large enterprises that could pay their own way while training new personnel.

- To create a basis for the industrialization of rural areas, allowing large private enterprises to show their capabilities, thus laying the groundwork for a future in which agriculture is fully transformed.

Government support is absolutely necessary to ensure the participation of private enterprises in the development projects. For the government to play its role effectively, all state structures that can in any way contribute to development must participate. The government must, essentially, assume the responsibility for seeing to it that all relevant public—and private—agencies make development their primary job. At the earliest stages of development, the government must extend its infrastructure to all areas of the country, especially to previously neglected regions, and focus on assisting in the development of the multiplicity of small production units, particularly family farms. Government field personnel should familiarize themselves with all communities, even the most isolated, and establish contact with all the producers in their respective areas of competence. The field worker should engage in frequent, honest, and open dialogue with the local population as an equal among equals.

During the early stages, while working intensely on the local level, development personnel must remain aware that local level activity fits into a broader, regional context. The region, as already mentioned, is a functional realm that is small enough for grassroots contact between the developer and the people but is also large enough to justify inter-sectional planning. When the agents of change become inaccessible to the average peasant worker, the regional boundaries have to be redrawn. As stated by Mennes, Tinbergen, and Waardenburg:

The subdivision of a country into regions remains an art rather than a piece of pure science, since a compromise must be found between various principles, none of which can be given a complete application.[8]

The principles to which they refer include the constraints imposed by the infrastructures of a society, particularly the institutional structures, which must be able to penetrate all places where development work is needed. The regional scope must, however, encompass a sufficiently broad spectrum of local level activity, so that when labor becomes redundant in agriculture, it can be reabsorbed in industry, the construction of regional centers, and the service sector.

The basic institutional unit of development in the earliest stages is the village. While the individual peasant family is the primary production unit in the economy, the peasants are dealt with collectively on the local level through the village. The full institutional power of the development effort thus must be brought to bear on the village, in order to assist it in the transition from subsistence agriculture to commercial farming. While all this is taking place at the village level, the town must function as an urbanized regional center, where redundant labor from agriculture can be retrained and then absorbed in the industrial and service sectors. As already discussed, this is achieved through diversification of the farm unit. Only when this goal is attained will the stage be set for another transformation of farming, that is the introduction of the specialized farm. The population of the regional town is composed essentially of (a) redundant workers from the villages, and (b) skilled workers and free professionals who have been introduced from outside the region to provide essential services.

The town will have to provide institutional support for both groups. Some institutional structures will have to provide support for the workers who are still rooted in the traditions of their parents and remain emotionally tied to their native village. A very different kind of institutional support structure is necessary for the urban skilled workers and professionals who are accustomed to the educational and cultural sophistication of the city and to a relatively high level of services and amenities.

The institutions devised to effect development change must be flexible since they must change and adapt as development occurs. Those who staff the institutional structures are responsible not only for initiating activity but must also communicate to the population and the development field workers the effects of what they are doing and how the changes brought about in one sphere of activity make further changes necessary. For example, the establishment of an industrial enterprise in a purely agricultural area will bring in workers who will need perishable foodstuffs such as vegetables, milk, meat, and eggs. This will mean the introduction of new crops into what was formerly subsistence farming, creating the diversification of farms and changing the agricultural sector. Another example is the construction of a road connecting an area suitable for the cultivation of sugar beets with a locale with a sugar mill, which will enhance the development of agriculture and industry.

JOBS TO BE DONE

The first task facing the nation's institutional structures is the establishment of the development campaign itself. For this purpose, the institutional structures must be treated as an all-encompassing, nation-wide endeavor requiring the full mobilization of every resource at the disposal of the society. Next comes heightening the consciousness of the masses, government agencies, and private groups. The principle of present sacrifices by the individual for the future welfare of the society must be introduced. Awareness of the role of government as the prime mover and partner of the people in the development campaign must be awakened. Propagation of the concept that all individuals in the nation, from the peasantry and proletariat to the free professionals and industrialists, hold an equal franchise in the development campaign is critically important.

The institutional machinery that will direct the growth process must be identifiable and should be presented as potent instruments of change worthy of confidence. The system of planning and implementation, the channels of communications, the points of accessibility, and the clear procedures to be followed throughout the growth program must be explained. The eventual changes that are anticipated as a result of growth should be described so that an *esprit de corps* is generated without arousing unrealistic expectations among the people involved.

When attempting to come to terms with the development campaign, the peasants readily understand development planning on the local level; they can also conceive of the national level, since they are accustomed to paying taxes, to being conscripted into the military, and to using the various national services. But in most cases, the peasant finds the concept of the region, as such, totally unfamiliar. Adding to the alien character of the regional level is the fact that it is the only level that will generally be defined by a novel set of institutional structures. The national role in development planning will be played by the existing ministries and other agencies; while local conditions change radically as a result of development, they do so through the transformation of structures familiar to the peasant, such as farms and villages. The introduction of previously nonexistent development structures occurs only on the regional level, and, therefore, one of the tasks of the development planner is to prepare the peasants for the changes ahead.

AN EXAMPLE OF DECENTRALIZATION IN ACTION

The Chinese example is a case where collectivized agrarian activity has come about through a decentralized, multi-level institutional framework.[9] The Chinese development program has been largely agrarian and collectivized. The early forerunners of the Chinese commune as it exists today were the Mutual Aid Teams. These consisted of a maximum of ten households that functioned as cooperatives, at first only during the peak harvesting seasons. Eventually, Agricultural Producers Cooperatives were created in which the management of land and other resources was cooperative, while particular plots of land remained privately owned, though available for collective use. From this stage of collectivization emerged the Chinese commune, in which all resources and means of production were collectivized, with only marginal household plots remaining under private ownership. Initially, the nascent communes incorporated 60-100 households, but by the late 1950s, the average commune included 5,000 households.

The size of the Chinese commune and some procedural issues were revised during the early 1960s, when a further decentralization, this time within the commune, came about. The commune was divided into brigades and the brigades into teams, with each level having control over particular areas and functions: the commune controlled land and large-scale workshops, etc., while the brigade controlled tractors, irrigation systems, and other means of production of a similar scale. The teams have control over the basic traditional tools of agriculture such as hoes, shovels, and axes.

The communes themselves are subdivisions of the *xian* level of functioning, which corresponds to the functional concept of the region, previously described. This system of multi-level decentralization has met with considerable success, and, according to Chung-Tong and Ip:

> The commune system . . . has provided a viable institutional framework for rural development in China. Ideally, under such an organizational arrangement, it is expected that a more rational management of agricultural production would be implemented. In agricultural production, manpower, labor, land and resources could be organized and utilized more efficiently and mobilized more effectively to benefit all members. . . . The commune structure was expected to demonstrate that, as agricultural production developed by improving resource endowments and consolidating the basis of agricultural production, it would develop pressures which would lead to the development of scientific and industrial programs. With increased agricultural production and growing rural surplus, a supporting infrastructure for rural development could be developed to produce new inputs of capital and skills necessary for further advances in agricultural production.[10]

From the point of view of feeding its population, Chinese agriculture has achieved many of its objectives. A large part of the credit for this achievement is due to the innovative and far-sighted institutional structures it has mobilized. In the Chinese case, decentralization takes place both within the commune and at the *xian* regional level.

In addition, multitudes of commercial outlets were established in the rural areas. The very creation of such enterprises attests to China's development progress. According to Jack Gray,[11] 90 percent of the communes and 80 percent of the labor brigades in Chinese rural areas have created some form of commercial enterprise. The presence of such entities is likely to be of great importance to the developing Chinese economy since there are nearly one and a half million of them. If the smaller-scale commercial ventures of mutual aid teams are also included, the numbers are even more staggering.

A LOOK AT THE NEW INSTITUTIONS

The Chinese example of successful decentralized development planning on a regional level is but one of many. My firsthand experience, supported by accounts such as the one above, make it clear that the concept of regional planning[12] as a cross-function can be used as a practical tool only if the institutions responsible for regional development can meet the following requirements:

- Continuous coordination on a regular basis among the various planners acting together as a team, and between them and those responsible for national level planning;
- Active and continuous relations between those involved in planning and those in charge of carrying out the plans in the various fields and sectors;
- Enough flexibility in development programs to ensure the possibility of transferring resources from one objective to another, as changes occur during the process of implementation;
- Active participation of the local population, leadership, and government agencies in order to mobilize local resources—public and private.

The ability to formulate and implement integrated development programs depends to a large extent on the ways in which the agencies and groups involved are organized. Since government cannot be entirely restructured to meet the needs of integrated regional development programs, development planners must set up an organization that can combine, or at least coordinate, the various government services in a region—a regional authority with sufficient power to coordinate, or in some cases even to take over, government functions within the region.

I am deliberately not setting up specific guidelines for the creation of such institutions. One thing my experience in the field has taught me is that the administrative structure of a regional authority assumes different forms in different countries. An authority may be needed for the development of a particular area, for example, a particularly backward or depressed area as in the case of the SUDENE regional authority, charged with the development of the northeast region of Brazil.[13] Another time, an agency will need to be set up to administer a rich area endowed with natural resources that can be exploited for the benefit of the nation as a whole. And another time, an agency may have to be created with the right mix of development experts to handle a sparsely populated area or one in which a new settlement scheme is planned, as in the case of Las Pirquitas in the Argentinian province of Catamarca.[14] It is often important that the authority be a separate institution granted a high degree of independence, able to interact directly with the central government in one way or another. This was the case, for example, in the creation of Sri Lanka's Gal-Oya Development Board,[15] which was set up as an independent body responsible to the Minister of Agriculture and Lands.

A different type of development authority is represented by the Settlement Department of the Jewish Agency for Israel, which is responsible for rural development in Israel. The Department, which operates on the national level, has five regional offices serving as the development authority for the areas under their jurisdiction. Most activities are carried out through the regional office closest to the actual site of the settlement project. These regional units are invested with the power to act independently, within certain limits, in accordance with the general policy laid down by the Central Board of Directors. Among their responsibilities are the provision of extension services and supervision of technical planning activities. The regional office has administrative and professional manpower, including planning, engineering, extension and guidance, and organization and budget units. The regional office thus forms a self-sufficient body, headed by a regional director.

The real measure of independence of the regional authority is not gauged by its administrative position but rather by its decision-making power in the spheres of planning and implementation. In the field of planning, experience in many countries, Israel among them, has shown that constant coordination between planning on the national and regional levels is a necessity. But since the national and regional authorities usually operate through different organizational channels, there must be a constant two-way flow of information, with draft plans going up and down the ladder of planning levels, before and even during implementation. For example, the institutional channels of information should run horizontally, say, between director-generals of the agricultural and industry ministries and vertically between them and the staff of the regional authority.

Based on my experience, I believe that the Regional Authority that serves as the operational arm of development activity in the field should consist of:

- The regional directorship, including the official and his or her bureau;
- The superintendents and coordinators of the regional development program;

• Two committees staffed by professionals, but guided according to policy that is formulated by a lay board. (The first of these is a planning committee, the other deals with coordination and implementation. The lay boards should be composed of representatives of every significant and organized force operating in the region, including delegates of corporations and peasants associations, research institutes, cooperatives, trade unions, and manufacturers associations.)

The Regional Development Planning Boards of Indonesia provide an example of decentralized regional development authorities. As described by MacAndrews, Sibero, and Fisher, a major goal of the

[Indonesian national development] plan . . . is the recognition of specific development problems and potentials in different regions, specific attention to backward regions, the increasing participation of the regions themselves in development planning, and the integration of all of the individual regions within the framework of the national economy. . . .[16]

The same authors describe how these Regional Boards gradually strengthen their role:

The Bappedas [regional planning boards] initially began as little more than symbolic structures in most provinces lacking adequate staff and facing considerable uncertainties on all sides as to their roles and capacity to take over the coordination of planning from other government departments. But from the beginning they played an important role in promoting regional development issues as well as giving legitimacy to regional development planning as a major government function. They were encouraged to grow gradually with the strengthening of their staff and the identification of ways they could become effectively involved in local area planning. With the increasing support of the provincial governors the position of the Bappedas by the late 1970s as the main coordinating unit for local area development at the provincial level was well-established.[17]

The Indonesian institutional structure, though not flawless, is similar to the kind of institutional network I am advocating. The region, under the guidance of a lay committee, but directed by a professional staff, is the base for operations of the regional effort to coordinate activities at the level of individual production units. While it is self-evident, it still needs to be stressed that the committee should be staffed by competent sensitive people who together provide expertise in such varied areas as, for example, community health, mechanical engineering, hydrology, construction work, accounting, agronomy. Coordinating this array of professionals—who must, in addition to special skills, have the ability and willingness to communicate their knowledge and see and communicate the effects of their efforts on the other work of the other specialities—is the responsibility of the director of the regional authority. There is a strong need for:

a new professional . . . we could designate as the "comprehensive development planner." The late Professor Ahumada called him a "specialist in generalization"; a title which indicates what is required of such a planner. He does not have to be an expert in any of the professional disciplines required in development planning. He must, however, know enough . . . to recognize the pattern of relationships between them and to weigh the mutual effects of the activities in each. . . .[18]

Such a development generalist is the type of individual needed to direct the development effort from the regional authority. This discipline may prove to be the most important in developing planning.

Since the regional authority serves as the catalyst for development activity, it requires economic means to effect development change and elicit cooperation from the participants in the development process. The funds that are made available to the regional authority, which should be the responsibility of the head of the agency, can be derived from a variety of sources. The government can simply decree that each regional authority be allocated a defined budget on a scale comparable to that of a national ministry. While maximizing the freedom of action of the regional authorities, such an approach to funding decreases the capability of the national government to monitor the use of allotted funds. A preferable approach requires that a defined part of each ministry's budget be transferred to the regional treasuries. This assures the ministries that the regional projects it has mandated as part of overall national plans will be implemented. The implementation itself, however, is an integral part of the regional development program directed by regional officials.

The institutional guidelines discussed thus far apply to the first two stages of the growth process. With the attainment of more advanced stages, field conditions change and so must the institutional structures. The expansion of production capacity, the increased accessibility of the means of production within an expanding geographical area, and the strengthening of private initiative effectively serve to diminish differences in conditions: progress will deemphasize the region as the focus of development activity.

THE CHANGING INSTITUTIONAL ROLE

At the earliest stages of development, the newly created institutional structures work most intensely at the village level, focusing on agrarian development. The priorities of the developers are to use labor resources that have been underutilized in subsistence agriculture and to maximize agricultural productivity. The goals of the developers are to increase the nation's ability to feed its masses and to generate surplus capital through marketing. Frequently, the first steps are extremely basic. For example, improving irrigation methods in the El-Sisal region of the Dominican Republic[19] was necessary before even rudimentary agricultural development could begin. Wells were deepened and siphons distributed to the peasants in order to utilize water resources by introducing the method of furrow irrigation instead of the traditional irrigation by flooding. In an effort to ensure that effective water resource management would become a permanent part of regional development, even after the departure of the technical experts who had been brought in by the planners, village "water committees," composed of four peasants elected to the posts, were set up. Lakashmanan provides another example of an innovative institutional structure created to promote development at an early stage in the process:

The Anand Milk Union Limited (AMUL) in Gujarat, India was set up, transcending local caste, class, or political schism, by creating a cooperative in a labor-intensive sector that gives a comparative advantage to small farmers and even those with little or no land. Collective ownership of the plant, democratic decisionmaking, cost-conscious management with quality control procedures and a homogeneous organization with a simple objective are the ingredients of a cooperative program which benefits the poor without directly affecting the well-off.[20]

As agricultural production structures expand and grow more sophisticated, other institutional frameworks become appropriate. The El-Sisal project used training farms in order to instruct local peasants in improved agricultural methods.[21] In Bas Boen, Haiti, when the development project began to prove successful, peasants who had chosen to remain wage-earning menial laborers when it began decided to join the project and to take on plots of their own.[22] In effect, the project convinced the peasants to become farmers. So, too, in less than a decade, the peasants of Kafubu and Kafulafuta in Zambia managed to move from primitive subsistence farming into productive, surplus-producing cooperative settlements, modeled after the Israeli family farms production cooperative.[23] It is important to remember that the first stage of satisfying the primary material needs for the entire population cannot be attained through the subsistence farm structure. Agricultural production should evolve out of subsistence to diversification, which is impossible if only the agricultural sector is changed; it requires simultaneous activity in the industrial and service sectors, activity that supports the transformation of agriculture.

As a society advances from the primary needs stage in preparation for the social competition stage, the emphasis in development planning changes from agriculture to industry. The support system geared toward agrarian activity must, however, remain in place as long as it is needed by the farmers; the development generalists are now freed to turn their attention to the regional towns and emerging service centers, as well as to agricultural villages. Instructors must be mobilized to train those no longer needed in agriculture for entry into industry and the services. The field staff at this stage have as their major tactical concern building worker and farmer cooperatives, which allow the individual farms to operate independently, without the constant support and direction of professional specialists.

The regional authority, at the initial phase of the social competition stage, remains more or less intact, although the lay committees assume greater influence over the professional planning teams and coordination committees. The regional authority steadily abdicates aspects of its various roles as the local villages, towns, and service centers set up institutional structures to replace them. At the national level, at this stage, planning begins to integrate activities between regions, and institutions are established to develop industrial activities, which are not dependent on or related to agriculture. The shift of emphasis to the industrial and service sectors should be fully implemented before society is ready to pass to the third stage, full affluence.

At the full affluence stage, the conditions on the local and regional levels change dramatically. The production system is capable of meeting demand, and the infrastructures provide accessibility to essential services on an increasingly uniform basis, eliminating most of the differences between metropolitan and rural regions. On the local level, development personnel in the field have all but been withdrawn. Village committees and town councils take on self-governing functions that have as their main aim the improvement of the quality of life rather than the provision of food, shelter, education, health care, and other primary material needs. Private enterprise, on the local and regional levels, is now almost free of public involvement in its affairs.

The development of the physical infrastructure, which is an absolute precondition for full integration of the regional networks into the national one, was achieved in the previous stage of development. The regions at full affluence are already integrated into the overall national picture, and the main economic activity passes from the region to the central government. At this point in my scenario of successful development, the closest body to a ministerial coordination committee, headed by the prime minister or his equivalent, is replaced by a newly created ministry of development. This ministry has as its main concern seeing to it that there is uniform national accessibility to production and services, bolstering any sector where development gains have been less than satisfactory. Greater emphasis will be placed on the quality of life in the nation as a whole and on ecological concerns. This ministry will be counseled by a lay advisory committee dealing with continuing problems of development, but its major concern will be preparing the nation to join international planning and development efforts. The institutional structure that was implemented to aid development will have evolved into an institutional structure of quite another kind. At this stage the question of values, especially basic values, is the overriding concern of society.

CHAPTER 7

THE SOCIAL DIMENSION

The social dimension of planning—the people, their willingness to embark on the development effort—is the critical force in development. Without the cooperation of the people in the area being developed, neither the ideas presented in the Development Frame of Reference, nor the Optimal Mix Principle, nor the construction of all the institutional structures in the world will be of any use. Thus, a social structure that encourages cooperation among the people involved in a project and between the people and the planners must be the primary goal of the development specialist.

PLANNING FOR AND WITH PEOPLE

Although many development planners disagree, I believe that traditional kinship patterns can be used to promote change in developing societies. The extended family kinship pattern—the tribe, clan, village, and similar social institutions—can be considered the basis of *communities of values.* Like oil, which can be used to move tractors, trucks, and earthmovers, or can be used to burn, destroy, and annihilate, these values can be a force for development, or they can be destructive. The job of the planner, first and foremost, is to ensure that these values work in his favor.

Admittedly, the community of values and its impact on development is difficult to isolate from all other variables, but the importance of maintaining communities of values has been strongly demonstrated by the Israeli experience and continues to be substantiated by circumstantial evidence in other countries. Therefore, I believe the time has come for the development planner to reevaluate the beliefs of such analysts as Fillol, who maintain that the extended family is one of the major impediments to economic growth.[1] Given the poor record of development specialists, planners should be more than ready to take a hard look at those values by which traditional society fulfills the basic existential needs of its members in order to determine how those values can be made an effective part of planning.

The family performs a variety of functions: it builds group identity (transmitted through the family and extended family), and it reinforces the individual's sense of belonging and continuity through a positive bond of affection, love, and admiration that are expressed in rites of passage and solidarity. Further, kinship ties bolster collective relations in society and place emphasis on group cooperation and individual sacrifice. (The land cultivated by a family for generations is often identified with kinship—sometimes in an extreme way—which can lead to diligence in protecting the environment and in engaging in productive labor.) The family also serves as a framework for economic cooperation in all or in some of its activities.

Owing to their power and fundamental importance, communities of values can be used as an instrument in the development process. I have, in fact, come to define development as economic growth *combined with* the social well-being that results from the preservation of communities of values. But the social components of development constitute the least understood and most neglected aspects of the process, and the political and economic problems facing all too many developing nations blur the issue.

While the people of the developing nations tenaciously attempt to cling to their traditions and families, the erosion of their traditional social structures has been rapid and brutal. The city is said to represent progress, yet the people of these poor nations find themselves socially devastated as a result of migration to metropolitan areas. Circumstances in the developing countries today are not the same as they were a century and a half ago when the cities of the developed nations were offering what seemed like unlimited employment opportunities. Modern geographical mobility is similar to that of the First Industrial Revolution, but it is not taking place at a time of occupational mobility created by improved and enlarged production methods. The different and extremely difficult conditions that prevail today result in a breakdown of the feeling of being a part of a community and substitute nothing for that loss. In a world in which everyone is aware of the disparities between rich and poor nations, this quickly creates an environment in which alienation and disaffection fester, and social unrest and revolt are easily provoked.

The social, political, cultural, and military gales that have rocked many of the developing nations are a result of the breakdown of basic values and discourage mass participation in the development process, participation that normally stems from the involvement, understanding, and partnership of the people and the authorities in the design and execution of development plans. Such popular mobilization requires a climate of security and widespread confidence in national community and its continuity. Belief in the national community and in its continuity, which are basic values, is a necessary antecedent to societal transformation, especially in rural areas, as has been shown in a number of studies.[2]

There is, of course, another set of values relative to the society in which an individual lives—social values, those that define status, norms, leadership, and achievement. Basic values should not be changed by development, but social values can and should change during the growth process. Naturally, there are times when the distinction between the two kinds of values systems is blurred as, for example, in a society that believes implicitly that its leadership rules by divine right, but basic values deal with transcendent concerns, those of the "City of God," and do not directly pertain to worldly concerns. Social values, on the other hand, affect and are affected by relations between individuals or classes in the society.

THE SOCIAL DIMENSION OF
AGRICULTURAL DEVELOPMENT

Perhaps one of the most damaging changes in social values in many countries, including many of the affluent, industrialized ones, is the lack of status accorded to those who work in agriculture. The First Industrial Revolution advanced humanity out of confining economic limitations. But instead of recognizing that a sound agricultural foundation had made the Industrial Revolution possible, people continued to see farmers and peasants as menial laborers involved in a branch of the economy with little status. In developing countries, this status problem runs in a vicious circle: The peasant's willingness to participate in a development project depends in part on his status which, in turn, depends on the success of his farm. The success of the farm is itself keyed to the status accorded agriculture in the national economic agenda.[3] In societies plagued by a surfeit of low-yield farms, farming itself is stigmatized.

This circle can be broken. The Israeli experience and that of many other developing nations shows clearly that the only way to proceed is by upgrading the status of agriculture in the eyes of the society. This is particularly pertinent in developing nations today because agriculture is the key in the first stage to higher economic achievement. The mass communications media—newspapers, radio, television—can be of great use in fostering increased status for farmers; the most important factor, though, is the government's official stand and the opinions expressed by its field representatives.

The success of rural development in Israel can undoubtedly be attributed in part to the high regard extended to agriculture in the values system of the Israeli society. The effect of this positive attitude is reflected in the large portion of resources allocated during the 1950s and 1960s to agricultural development, in the quality of development personnel, in the activist stance of farmers associations, and, ultimately, in the response of peasants and farmers to the development program. The significance of this change of attitude was also observed in Haiti.[4] When the peasant in Bas Boen realized that the social worth of his occupation increased as a result of improved methods of production, a visible change in production, bolstered by motivation, was observed.

It is difficult to prove "scientifically" that social resources are the key to the success of development activity because of the paucity of data relating to social structures,* but the power of social factors has been demonstrated time and again to those engaged in field work. Nowhere, perhaps, has this been better documented than in the Israeli experience.[5]

---

*Since social factors cannot be quantified and no methodology has yet been created to measure the effect of such factors on the development process, many plans pay lip-service to them without treating them to any practical degree.

Two villages, A and B, were established at the same time and situated side by side in the southern region of Israel. The natural resources available to them were identical, and their settlers came from the same part of North Africa. Each village consisted of approximately sixty farms, and each farm was allocated the same amount of land, water, and means of production. There was every reason to expect both villages to develop along the same lines.

Village A developed rapidly. Formerly merchants and artisans, such as cobblers and metalsmiths, the settlers adapted to the rural way of life, which they had not known before, in a relatively short time. Although they required considerable professional advice and assistance during the first years of farming, the villagers of Settlement A were able to achieve a steadily rising yield and income, and they found their new lives increasingly satisfactory.

Village B, on the other hand, kept lagging behind. After eight years it was still a backward settlement with only a few productive farmers. Some families left the village, and most who stayed had to make their living from a variety of odd jobs. Of the forty-eight families who inhabited the village in 1960, only eighteen earned their living entirely from farming; nineteen others did not cultivate their holdings at all.

Social research conducted in the two villages brought to light the reason for the startling discrepancy in their economic growth and quality of life. Village A was inhabited mostly by interrelated families, and their leadership structure had remained largely intact. Consequently, these settlers exhibited feelings of solidarity and a readiness to assist one another. The leadership of Village A cooperated with the development authorities and proved instrumental in helping the settlers adapt to modern agricultural methods.

Village B, which was composed of a number of different kinship groups, lacked a single, recognized leadership. The leaders of the various groups frequently operated at cross-purposes, so that new institutions could not be established or function with any measure of permanence and authority. The divisions in leadership sapped the energies of the settlers and diluted all incentives for communal development. The breadwinners of the village found themselves incapable of providing for their families, and many sought their livelihoods outside of the village.

It was evident that proving adequate means of production could not by itself generate economic success in the twin villages. Furthermore, the social factor was not recognized until well after the settlements had been established. In the case of Village B, development authorities were compelled to change their original plans. Families with no extended kinship ties were resettled outside the village and were replaced by families who had relatives there. Eventually, success was achieved in Village B.

Direct evidence of the influence exerted by social structures on development is rare. However, in Israel it has invariably been found that channeling forces intrinsic to established kinship patterns and communities of values brings positive results. Israel represents a unique instance wherein entire communities have been resettled *in toto*, thereby preserving social patterns. But there is also a wealth of circumstantial evidence from other parts of the world showing that mobilizing communities of values to support development activities can prove decisive to development success.

The social dimension of development can be operationally treated by planning for "communities of values," that is, relatively small societal organisms, basically comprised of interrelated families and extended kinship patterns that "develop from within." The reasons that communities of values remain so entrenched and cohesive should constitute a field of inquiry in itself. There are, though, several factors that can immediately be discerned. Specific communities of values in rural areas of developing countries lead to people identifying with lands that they regard as ancestral. Their spatial milieu is the same as that of their forebearers and has assumed a central role in the mythos of the community. The very terrain and natural environment of the community form the foundation on which all communal activity—economic, social, and cultural—takes place.

The Chinese have recognized the importance of communities of values to development, and they have refined their program for economic growth accordingly. As described by Chung-Tong and Ip:

Since 1979, the production unit has had full autonomy to decide on how to organize the available manpower to increase productivity and the quality of production. The *pai gong* (work assignment) system in which larger tasks were assigned to work groups on a rotation basis or permanent responsibility for smaller tasks given to a small group of members, still prevalent in many places, is beginning to be replaced by the system of *bao gong* (fixing work). . . . The advantage of the *bao gong* system, according to the peasants, is that the small work group could be formed on the basis of personal ties, residential contiguity, or kinship relations. . . .[6]

Once the importance of communities of values for the development process is accepted, an adequate system of social relations must be formulated to set out the rights and responsibilities of the society and of the individual during the development process. Such a system must utilize communities of values and values systems as a fulcrum for development participation. These relations can be formalized in a social pact that can be used to explain the development process clearly to the entire society.

THE SOCIAL PACT AND DEVELOPMENT

All societies, from pastoral clans of hunters and gatherers to sophisticated and complex industrialized nations, operate according to an implicit social pact. Whether unwritten or enshrined in fanciful documents, a set of rules governs the relationship between the individuals in a society. Power is given to a leader or governing body in exchange for providing the individual's social needs.

The social pact must play a central role in development planning. During periods of social equilibrium, social pacts remain stable and unchanging for long periods. During development, however, the social pact changes with each stage in the growth process, and different societal conditions are required at each level of functioning. An example of a development social pact is that of the Community Development Program of India, as discussed by Anand Sarup, who notes that the "cardinal principles" of India's Community Development Program were formulated prior to its independence.[7]

Chung-Tong and Ip describe a similar approach, but one more limited in scope than the Indian Community Development Program:

The size, ownership structure and functions of the communes were changed substantially in a series of decisions beginning at the end of 1960, which culminated in the publication of the "Draft Regulations Concerning the Rural Communes," commonly known as the "Sixty Articles," in 1962. This document detailed the responsibilities and rights of the members of the commune, and the organizational structure for decision making, management and planning. . . . Brigade boundaries were redrawn to reflect natural and historical features and to conform with customary kinship ties, trading patterns and mutual aid networks. Teams were reorganized with member households who were on good terms with each other.[8]

The social pact between society and the individual evolves during the development process, and although the ways in which the individual's social needs are met can vary from one society to another, they must always be fulfilled. Society can demand the participation of the people in development only in return for meeting their social needs.

Social needs, as they apply to developing societies in the midst of their effort to structurally change the socioeconomic base of the country, should be viewed as consisting of the right of the individual to:

- the security and constancy of public order;
- a franchise in the economic system equal to that held by all others;
- a personal voice in the decisionmaking process; and
- a say in decisions affecting personal environment.

Although the manner in which society meets social needs is a function of cultural and other influences unique to the society, each developing society should aim at meeting these needs. The purpose of the social pact is to define the mutual responsibilities and rights of society and its members. While the development social pact constitutes a kind of "bill of rights" for the individual, it also defines the nature of mass participation in development. The social pact must not only set out the nature of mass participation, it must also define the means by which popular mobilization in development is achieved: coercion or consensus.

Events in developing countries have consistently shown that no amount of coercion can subdue the wrath of oppressed people for long. A government can dominate a nation by the use of strong-arm tactics for a time, but authoritarian regimes cannot long prevail without disruption. People in the developing world now seek greater control over their lives, and the only way a regime can establish a successful development program is to mobilize the people through consensus. The examples of what happens when consensus is ignored are many: Poland, Afghanistan, Iran, Brazil, Vietnam, the Philippines, Nicaragua, and El Salvador.

Development consensus necessarily involves mass participation. However, since social factors have been so neglected in the study of development, there is little theory to guide policymakers in securing development participation among the masses. J. M. Cohen and N. T. Uphoff have pointed out that:

Unfortunately, there is little systematic knowledge to draw on in the social sciences concerning *development* participation. Indeed, there is even little consensus on what constitutes *political* participation, despite much more work and writing on that subject.[9]

The difference between political conformity and development consensus means that government and the individual need not concur on political issues in order to cooperate in development. The emergency presented by the development challenge makes political issues of secondary importance on the national agenda. The social pact does not require that the partners entering into this contract agree on matters outside the development domain. It does, however, demand that the social rights of the individual be compatible with development consensus and participation.

There are, of course, limits to the distinctions between political conformity and development consensus. Establishing and maintaining the development authorities as the power center of a developing nation will inevitably alienate certain sectors of the population. Those most likely to protest the intense development regime will generally be the elite classes in the society whose opposition to development is a result of their fear that it will cost them their privileged position. Development authorities, however, cannot permit themselves to pander to special interest groups, such as the military, landowners, or clerics, despite their strength. During the early stages in the growth process, I firmly believe that development authorities must have full access to all national resources, including those held in private hands. There will come a time, assuming that development is successful, when the individual will be given free rein to assert himself economically. In the interim, though, individuals in developing societies are entitled to have their primary material, existential, and social needs fulfilled, and elite interests should not be allowed to supersede the needs of the nation as a whole.*

While there is no agreement among development specialists concerning the nature of development participation, there is widespread recognition that mass involvement is necessary to attain development. This realization has been increasingly accepted of late, as reflected, for example, in the following resolution passed by the United States Congress:

Unless the people benefit from development efforts, no meaningful progress can result from foreign aid. . . . The great potential for planning and implementation of development activities, contained in the mass of the people in the developing countries, is still largely untapped, which slows down the achievement of the objectives of the foreign assistance program.[10]

MASS PARTICIPATION

In their analysis of the role of mass participation in rural development, Cohen and Uphoff[11] point out that the nature of popular mobilization has been debated, without consensus, since Aristotle. It is clear, though, that mass mobilization for development is not tied to a particular kind of government, that is, there is no single "correct" form of government for development. Constructive development activity can be and has been attained under a wide variety of regimes, as can be seen by looking at the

---

*I can here only express my disappointment that the governments of Israel in the late seventies and early eighties did not realize that Israeli society had passed from the first development stage, primary needs, to the second one, social competition, and alter the optimal mix accordingly. This resulted in paternalism toward private initiative, which assisted the privileged rather than the needy. This, I believe, is the cause of our present crisis, to say nothing of the huge expense involved in unnecessary and harmful military adventures.

diversity, indeed the divergence, of states in which development progress has been achieved.

In Taiwan and Spain, for example, where right-wing regimes controlled the state structures during much of the growth process in the post-World War II period, development was advanced. Franco's Spain was the site of one of the most comprehensive land reform programs ever instituted in Europe, and the gains were made through extensive formal consultations between government officials and representatives of the local population in developing areas. Similarly, the reactionary Chaing Kai-shek, having been exiled from the Mainland where he had championed the interests of major landowners against those of peasants, effected an extensive land reform program on decentralized lines in Formosa. Chaing's motives in instituting land reform were, of course, political. Nonetheless, the reform program was successful from the development point of view.

At the center of the political spectrum, social democratic regimes in Japan have been among the most successful in instituting sound and lasting development change. Japan established a comprehensive supporting infrastructure which paved the way for far-reaching economic growth. Japan's growth program advanced the country from economic ruin to the pinnacle of industrial affluence in less than two generations. Similar progress in economic growth was achieved by Israel under the Labor governments that were in power from 1948 to 1977.

On the left, Communist countries such as China and Yugoslavia have also achieved impressive economic growth. Since 1953, when Yugoslavia embarked on a separate development program from that of the rest of the Eastern bloc, it has maintained a strict separation between political and development activities. Politically, Yugoslavia has remained highly centralized. In the economic sphere, though, Yugoslavia represents one of the world's best examples of decentralized decisionmaking.

The People's Republic of China offers a striking example of mass participation in development. Politically, China operates as a dictatorship, ruled from the center. In terms of economic decisionmaking, though, China has displayed a far-reaching degree of decentralization. Also, the mobilization of the masses in China has been virtually all-encompassing: throughout the country the population is abuzz with the work of development. Further, the Chinese region, the *xian*, the functional level at which most of the daily decisionmaking and implementation take place, is the level at which delegates of the local population and government representatives hammer out budgets, plans, and procedures. The regional approach to development applies not only to its villages but also to the regional towns. It thereby covers most of the territorial expanse of this vast country, excluding the metropolitan areas. This is correct given China's current development status, which is at the late primary material needs stage, when all development activity should be geared toward meeting minimal food, shelter, medical, and educational needs.

The lesson of these examples is that development can advance under a variety of political regimes, including some that are widely divergent with regard to ideology and politico-military policy. What is common to all of these nations is a stable social order. And they all regard development as an urgent task requiring the cooperation of the government, special interest groups, and the people.

Common to the above countries and, according to research done in Israel,* to all nations that have made development progress, is mass participation in development activity. The nature of this participation and the way in which it is enlisted differ from society to society. The term "participation" embraces a broad set of attitudes, behavior patterns, and activities. It is not, however, a one-time act that can be dispatched by dropping a ballot into a polling box. Participation is a process that must fully involve as many people as possible in both the rural and urban areas.

The Chinese development experience is instructive in a number of respects. Prior to, during, and since the Cultural Revolution, the Chinese communicated development aims directly to the people through wall posters, newspapers, broadcast media, and mass meetings held in factories, on farms, and elsewhere. The authorities also made effective and abundant use of slogans such as: "Take grain as the key link,"[12] that is, apply yourself to intensive agricultural pursuits, and "A member of a commune is responsible for the quality of his work."[13] The Chinese have emphasized the

---

*Again, I am referring to the Rehovot team's work, which is described in the Preface.

importance of "local autonomy" in developing areas, where they have sought to "employ measures suitable to local conditions."[14]

Heightening the consciousness of the masses concerning the scope and nature of the development campaign constitutes the first step in creating mass participation. There can be no mistake about the limits imposed on mass involvement in the decisionmaking process during the early stages of development: the challenge is so complex and formidable, and the capabilities of the people so debilitated, that the initiative and responsibility for formulating policy and guidelines must be taken by the development authorities, but the people can and should be consulted and heeded as much as possible. For example, when there is a choice to be made about whether a particular village should cultivate rice or cotton, the importance of this decision in the overall development strategem of the nation may be marginal, but for the people whose livelihoods will depend on a dramatic change in the mode of agriculture they practice, the choice between rice and cotton represents a monumental issue.

My experience is that cooperative frameworks offer the best means to help peasants become farmers. They make production more efficient; they expand the opportunities to acquire new technology and equipment that is too costly for the individual farmer to obtain himself; and they serve to transform a community of small-scale farmers into a significant economic bloc for dealing with suppliers and markets.[15]

Sometimes, though, social conditions will work against the egalitarianism of a cooperative framework. For instance, Joseph S. Zalmanov, reporting on the El-Sisal Development Project in the Dominican Republic writes:

The program has been managed by a very competent Dominican Agrarian Reform team in conjunction with a small number of Israeli advisors. Although formal organizational structure for future cooperative management exists . . . as of 1971 the settlers have as yet taken no part in decisions. There is no lack of desire on the part of both the Agrarian Reform people and, certainly, the Israelis, to encourage cooperative development but the deeply rooted individualism and lack of tradition have thus far not been conducive to progress in this sphere.[16]

This represents a case where social values—not basic existential values—had to be overcome, patiently and sensitively, through education and persuasion—not force—for development progress to take place.

Planners working in Zambia found that while indigenous social values were inclined toward a spirit of cooperation between people, the low level of social development caused a premature attempt at collectivization to fail.[17] A happier experience was reported concerning the extremely underdeveloped region of Bas Boen in Valley Cul-de-Sac, Haiti, where development efforts led rather quickly to a cooperative and volunteering spirit.[18]

The concept of deferred gratification and collective effort and cooperation, as required by collectives and cooperatives, can be accepted by peasants and other workers. It is easy to instill the people with the expectation that their struggle will bring them ongoing benefits, but development authorities must operate forthrightly, carefully explaining that the benefits will not be immediate. The arduousness of the campaign and the time it will take before concrete gains are realized must be made clear to the people from the very beginning of the development enterprise; at the same time, hope in the future must be kept alive.

THE TACTICAL ROLE OF SOCIAL INFRASTRUCTURES

The design and execution of development projects and activities involving social infrastructures is the domain of social planning. When compared to economic, spatial, and institutional planning, social planning would seem to be a less sophisticated discipline. This misconception arises because although it is generally agreed that social structures have some effect on development, the extent of that effect continues to be the subject of much debate. Consequently, little effort has been made to systematically analyze anthropological, sociological, psychological, and other data relevant to development. In addition, because social planning deals with emotions, sentiments, traditions, lifestyles, and social groups, it largely relies on the personal experiences and insights of the specialists. The social planner often depends on intuition as much as knowledge; there is no laboratory distinct from actual field conditions in which social planners can practice their skills. Social planners are not concerned with crops and manufactured goods, steel and concrete; their concern is other human beings.

Throughout the development process, social planners are involved in four basic functions of equal importance: (1) sociological investigation—akin to the surveys by economists or physical planners prior to the formulation of plans—of existing social groups and relations; (2) participation in the planning team—standing up for social factors (preventing their eclipse by economic considerations) and suggesting how they can be used to further economic growth; (3) serving as an information officer— explaining the goals and anticipated course of development to the people, and; (4) fulfilling the role of social engineer and ombudsman during the course of implementation.

As a sociological investigator, the social planner seeks information about indigenous power structures, intergroup relations, recognized native leadership, group cultural traits, and matters of daily routine in which members of the community engage. The planner then studies the history and traditions of the target population: its responses to such exogenous intrusions as war, natural disaster, and modern innovations. Once this is done, the social planner must spend as much time as possible with the people in their own environment in order to fully assimilate their worldview, language, religion, dress, diet, music, and folkways. The social planner then contributes this knowledge to the planning team as a whole.

Every aspect of social life, from the direction new houses will face, to the nature of inter-ethnic relations, must be reviewed in order to make them compatible with the ways of the target population. Prives, in his Zambian study, describes the emergence and resolution of inter-ethnic tensions and other strains in the social fabric ensuing from development resettlement.[19]

During the actual implementation of development projects, the social planner returns to the field and sees to it that the material uncovered in his investigation is taken into account in everyday planning. In this capacity, the social planner is concerned with more than the final product of development. If manual labor is forbidden to the target group on a given day of the week, the social planner must be sure that this injunction is taken into account in the development project. If a certain facility is needed for a given rite of passage practiced by the population, the social planner must see to it that such a facility is provided. It is up to the social planner to ensure that the development process becomes an integral part of the society.

The social planner must also assist the other professionals involved in development projects; nowhere is social psychology part of the college curriculum leading to an engineering degree, and most agronomists lack training in human sociology. Therefore, the social planner must be capable of counseling other development professionals whenever appropriate.

The role of the social planner as an information officer gradually becomes transformed into that of educator and trainer. The development enterprise constitutes a profound educational experience for everyone in the target society, from the toddler to the octogenarian— including the development officials themselves. For instance, as a result of the progress brought about by a development project in Zambia, women in the Kafubu and Kafulafuta areas began demanding a greater involvement in the decisionmaking process.[20] In matters such as this, the social planner *qua* educator must help developing communities find answers to issues that did not exist before the growth process began. Throughout most of the development implementation, the flow of information runs from the professionals to the people. However, whenever development officials cease to learn more about the people whose lives they are influencing, the growth process is doomed to failure.

Development education and training progresses from explanations and motivation to imparting concrete skills. A strategic goal of development is the increased independence of the people. In the Bas Boen, Haiti project, planners worked to make the community as self-reliant as possible. This goal was achieved within a relatively short period—little more than a decade.[21] As a result, the foreign experts were able to transfer management functions and withdraw from the project with the knowledge that the people were capable of taking over.

The target population must learn by doing and must be encouraged to do as much as possible for themselves, as soon as possible. Training becomes particularly important in preparing the peasants for the transition from the primary needs to the social competition stage. During the later stage workers displaced from agriculture will have to be reabsorbed in industry, which is a totally new and strange form of economic activity for them. Training for industrial activity is of great importance during the first stages of development, and it is up to the social planner to make sure that the people come to see the new production methods and technology as valued tools, not as impositions.

Changes in the peasants' mode of production inevitably alters the total sphere of family life. Nutrition, housing, education, clothing, and recreational needs evolve as a result of development. Infant mortality rates decline and the number of children born to the average family also changes. The social planner must predict and explain these changes to the population before they occur. The social planners and their community workers must employ every means available to assist the target population to adapt to the new conditions to ensure long-term development.

When involving entire communities in development, the social planner must be capable of using existing social relations advantageously. If the community accepts only the authority of religious or tribal leaders, then these leaders should be consulted and asked to endorse the development of their villages. For example, in the development projects in the Zambian copperbelt, the intervention of a tribal leader was solicited by the planners, and it later proved indispensible to the success of their development program.

Experience in Israel has shown that any attempt by the development authorities to undermine the authority of local leadership is likely to result in undesirable situations. For example, people from a Middle Eastern country were settled in a village in the northern part of the country. Their leader had already headed the community in its country of origin. A relationship of mutual respect existed between the leader and the staff of the regional office of the development authority. The village began to show economic progress, and after a time, new instructors came to the village. They were second-generation members of established cooperative villages, and they had the necessary professional qualifications to instruct the new farmers.

The instructors urged the settlers to adopt cooperative organization as practiced in the veteran socialist villages of the country. They emphasized the importance of establishing a village council that would run the village affairs according to accepted procedures. This endeavor undermined the authority of the local leader and resulted in a serious conflict among the settlers. Eventually, the leader began to lose his authority; the community, which had previously been stable, broke into different groups. The leader decided to leave the village, and with him went the core of the community. The village became a total failure.

Understanding the social background of the population is especially important in settlement areas where development authorities select the settlers. Such selection can be made by two methods. One way is based on the personal qualifications of candidates; the criteria are usually the potential to be successful farmers, a certain technical know-how and diligence, and, occasionally, the possession of a certain amount of capital. This method was used in choosing settlers for the Polders in Holland, for the Badajoz project in Spain, and for the Gal-Oya region in Sri Lanka. The basic weakness of this method when adopted for developing countries is that it ignores a social feature common to most traditional societies, that is, the existence of the kinship group as the basic social pattern. Selection of settlers on a personal basis proved to be the most adequate and efficient method for projects in the second stage of development. (An outstanding example is Holland's Polder projects.)

In developing countries, it is preferable to transfer complete communities from an old location to a new one. The main advantage of this method is that the uprooted community retains its social structures, thereby giving each individual a feeling of confidence, especially in the difficult early stages of adjustment that tend to determine the fate of the whole development project. The benefits of this approach outweigh the disadvantages of giving over part of the new resources to settlers who do not have the ability to exploit them with maximum efficiency as would be the case when choosing for skills and so forth.

In conclusion, I can state firmly that the social planner who is successful harmonizes the needs of economic growth with the capabilities, interests, and aspirations of the people involved in development. Therefore, the cardinal rule is that social planners cannot afford to isolate themselves from the people they are to serve. Sensitivity to the abilities and sensibilities of the people is the key to success. In the Bas Boen, Haiti project, planners had to do away with even simple bookkeeping since the illiterate population could not cope with such, for them, sophisticated methods. So the planners instituted a system of "internal money," whereby peasants "paid" for the supplies and engaged in other financial transactions by remitting or receiving chits.[22]

This highlights the social planner's general rule that if there is a conflict between the abilities of the people and a development project, it is the project that must be changed, not the people. For the social planner, the dignity of the population must always be upheld, and their communities of values must be respected and accommodated. Never forget that the success of a development program is the only lever that can bring about the social changes required in the second stage of the development process. Nothing else is capable of doing so.

CHAPTER 8

WAGING THE DEVELOPMENT STRUGGLE

The previous chapters define the scope of the development challenge and put forth some tools for the use of the development specialist based on the principles of the optimal mix, uniform accessibility, popular participation in development, and the multidimensionality of development. These tools are an outgrowth of my theory of development, which includes a belief in the importance of "communities of values," the societal frameworks within which people live; these are composed of kinship patterns and other traditional social structures that individuals are born, raised, work, and die within and through which, with little or no awareness, they make sense of their existence through religion, rites, myths, and folkways. Breaking with the conventions that have traditionally informed development activity, I maintain that communities of values should be considered the building blocks of development progress and socioeconomic change.

My theory aims at helping the development planner achieve two things: the economic growth of the society he is working with, and the distribution of existing national resources and newly attained wealth within the society in a manner that aids the maximum number of economically distressed people in that society. A major underpinning of my theory of development is a refutation of ideological bias when attempting to effect economic growth, since virtually all economic systems include both public and private spheres. Despite the raging ideological battle between proponents of the capitalist and marxist schools, the mixed economy approach serves as the basis of current realities throughout the world.

Of course, I have a bias toward the value of a mixed economy: Israel has had a mixed economy since its independence, when it was truly a developing country. Israel today is close to being a wholly developed nation. Israeli planners have also been successful in implementing mixed economies in the field in developing countries. For example, a development plan formulated by a joint Greek-Israeli team for Crete was based on a mixed economy; the Greek government invested ten drachmas for every eight placed into the development regions by the private sector.[1] In agriculture, it prepared the way for land consolidation so that farming could become mechanized on integral family farms as opposed to the segmented plots of the traditional system. An ambitious irrigation program was instituted and a project was implemented to foster the development of industry so that jobs would become available for farm workers as they found themselves unemployed because of increased agricultural productivity. The plans also called for the modest expansion of the service sector in the form of a nascent tourist industry. After only a few years, it became clear that the ten-year Crete development program was succeeding.

The mixed economy program in Crete primarily limited government involvement to building infrastructures, providing services, and facilitating the involvement of the private sector in building productive capability. In this example, the mixed economy perspective proved capable of developing a particularly economically distressed region. But a mixed economy is not the only prerequisite to economic growth today: an integrated regional approach is also required. In this connection, R. Carrillo-Arronte and V. Grossman write of the Mexican experience that: "The legitimate and active participation of the regions in the progress of the country can only be sustained through integral and planned action."[2]

Planned action—planning—is based on the systematic deployment of human, institutional, and material resources. Planning must be comprehensive and, as such, it should be inter-sectoral and interdisciplinary, that is, integrated. Integrated development planning does not mean that equal weight is given to each sector throughout the development process, nor does the mixed economy component imply that private and public forces are to be equally applied at all times. Perhaps the most difficult of all planning functions is knowing when and to what extent a particular sector should be developed and which combination of the public or private forces will maximize the long-term social and economic returns of the development program. Primarily, development planners have had to rely on subjective experience and intuition. Therefore, the results inevitably have been inconsistent.

The integrated, interdisciplinary regional approach to development based on the concept of mixed economy may provide a road to development that can help the poverty-stricken masses of the world. The question is whether this road to development will actually be traveled. It is not enough to have the potential for alleviating poverty if contemporary decisionmakers fail to take their nations down that road.

NEW TOOLS FOR THE BATTLE AHEAD

While the integrated regional approach has been practiced to varying degrees in projects across the developing world during the past quarter of a century, the application of the approach to field realities has been far from easy. Coordinating governmental and private forces in the economy in a way that can meet existing needs while planning for future ones is an extremely formidable task involving a host of professional disciplines, tactics, tools, materials, and administrative frameworks.

If there is a silver lining behind the storm clouds in the developing countries today, it is the fact that an arsenal of weapons is available for the development struggle. In addition to specialists who have learned from both the economic growth process that took place in the now developed nations and from early work done to aid less developed nations, new technologies have been developed that are now widely available and can be used by the development specialist in his work. I would like to emphasize, in particular, the computer, which can be directly and concretely applied to the most difficult parts of the planning and implementation processes. The many uses that the development planner can find for the computer are evident in the complicated structures involved in integrated development planning.

Integrated planning requires:

- An interdisciplinary team functioning at each level of society. These teams should include economists, sociologists, physical planners, and a development planner who will usually serve as the head of such a team. All of these specialists should be well trained in their specific disciplines yet able to function as a team working to produce integrated planning in full detail.*

- A network of planning teams covering all of the regions of a country. These regional teams will communicate directly and continuously with a central team in the capital city. The team in the capital is responsible for national development planning based on dialogues between the national and regional level teams.

- A feedback relationship between planning and implementation that allows development activity to be constantly revised to conform to field realities. This requires the development specialists to constantly update data, logistics, and plans. Repeated updating requires consultation, data gathering and processing, forecasting, model development, and simulation.

In the past, meeting these requirements meant that a large number of equally experienced specialists had to be available to work in the field and in the regional and national centers. Constant evaluations of each step of a plan must be made in every area being developed, then analyses of the new information in terms of the progress in every other area and in terms of the plan as originally structured have to be prepared. The original plan then has to be adapted to the new field realities. Essentially, the planners are engaged in a series of repetitions involving constantly changing figures—for the different sectors of the same region, for the regions in relation to one another, and for the national plan as development progresses.

The continuous evaluations and the analyses and projections based on them, which are necessary if planning and implementation are to be successful, have been carried out in developing countries, but on a limited scale because of their dependence on

---

*The Rehovot Settlement Centre has been training such teams for more than fifteen years, and they have had success in the field in developing nations.

manually operated systems. Before integrated regional development planning can be done on a large scale, a number of difficulties will have to be met:

- The need for accurate memory and skills at comparison for performing the evaluations; the degree of expertise and experience and the amount of time needed to perform the analyses and projections based on the evaluations.

- The need to train enough specialists to do these operations (and the costs of the training).

- The need to settle on a single plan for each stage, although the team may discuss several alternatives. This may mean discarding alternatives that might, if worked out fully, prove more beneficial. (Personalities come into play here: a stronger voice, more charisma, greater seniority all can affect which alternative is chosen.)

- The need to present the development plan as a fixed document. Because development plans are often presented in the form of voluminous books, including maps, tables, and detailed analyses, they do not readily show how they can be adapted when situations change. Moreover, policymakers tend not to go through such voluminous books, and as a result, they do not become familiar with the main features of projects dependent on their decisions.

Over the past few years, I have been working with the Rehovot Settlement Study Centre planning team to find ways to use computer technology to meet these needs. We joined forces with the International Business Machines (IBM) Scientific Center in Haifa, Israel, to build a man-machine system that will overcome these difficulties. The system includes a comparative data bank and programs that allow most data to be easily presented in the form of charts, diagrams, and maps. The area that presents the most difficulty is the processing of non-quantifiable factors, such as the relation of social structures and human resources; these social factors will have to be clearly represented in the system and their influence on and links with other aspects of development plans must be convincingly conveyed. Another problem is ecological conditions, but if these can be identified in terms of their influence on land use, agriculture, types of housing, and so on, they too can be handled by a man-machine system. A computerized man-machine system for the regional level can be represented in the following way:

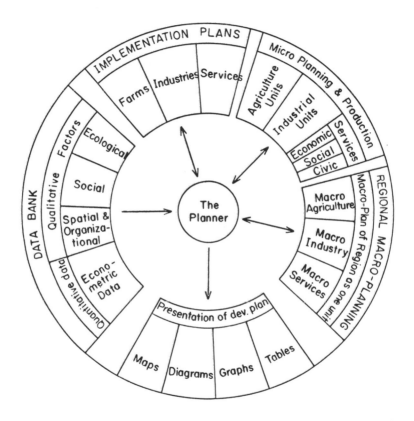

This system, which is being tested in pilot countries in Africa and Latin America, will enable development planners working in a capital city to coordinate development throughout the country by setting up a regional network. Personal portable computers will be the heart of the system, allowing disks with new data and analyses to be transported to other teams and to the capital quickly and easily. The material from each field team can be coordinated in the capital, and new directives taking numerous differences from the original plans into account can be quickly prepared.

But the new system offers more than speed. It allows the planner in the field, dealing with policymakers who might prefer different approaches, to feed the new approaches into the model and instantly display the results, instead of preparing second and third models in the old, time-consuming manner. I know how important this can be from firsthand experience.

A cabinet minister in a neighboring Middle Eastern country strenuously objected to a development plan I presented because he had promised the leaders of the region involved that a dam would be built on the river to collect the winter flows for use in irrigating the summer crops. He asked why I had not included such a project in the development plan I presented. As a matter of fact, the Rehovot team and I had analyzed the effects of building such a dam, but we decided that it would not be the best solution. Not only would it absorb most of the resources available for development in the region and take many years to build, but once built, the water would collect in large quantities and it would take many more years and additional funds to develop the means to bring it safely to all areas in the region. Our calculations had revealed that a gradual dispersed system of water sources, using smaller dams, borings for underground water, and dikes, would take much less time to construct and would be operational in stages while providing a better return on the investment. Of course, we had not done formal presentations for each plan because of the time involved in preparing such materials—each plan required different infrastructures, support systems, and layouts for new villages and towns. (Feeding the new information into an established computer program and having it calculate the results is infinitely faster.) If we could have given him the calculations based on each plan, clearly spelled out in charts and graphs, he might have had the incentive to argue with the leaders, showing them that he had found a quicker and cheaper solution. The large dam could be built later, when the system would be more mature and could afford it. The result was a decision to build the large dam—a project that has yet to be completed and that has curtailed overall development in the region.

THE DEVELOPMENT RESPONSIBILITY
OF POLICYMAKERS

To a large extent, the basic question of development planning is not whether integrated regional development is possible—clearly, I believe that it is—but whether policymakers are willing to adopt it, with all of its implications for the political structure. The case for adoption is a strong one and the alternatives far too costly. It is impossible either to accept the status quo (which only perpetuates socioeconomic and eventually political turmoil as the pressures from hopeless poverty build) or pursue conventional development planning (which has all too often failed in the past with the same disastrous results). To illustrate the need for successful development, even at the cost of decentralization and greater decisionmaking power being given to the people (a cost many leaders are unwilling to pay), I can point to the fate of Nicaragua's Samoza, Uganda's Amin—and the Shah of Iran.

The last is a case in which, again, I can speak from firsthand experience. In the early 1970s, the Emperor of Iran, the late Mohammed Pahlevi, realized that Iranian development was not working. He concluded that without a radical decentralization of government development operations in the field, progress would not occur. And so he issued a royal decree allocating 60 percent of the national development budget (a considerable figure in those days because of Iran's oil income) to the direct use of the local governments at the provincial level, to be under the control of governors appointed personally by him.

This decision was backed by the United Nations Development Program, and the UN's Center for Research and Training in Regional Planning was called on to assist in the implementation of this new development plan. To aid the plan, in 1974 a seminar and international panel of experts were set up to propose ways of implementing the new policy. I was a member and then part of a delegation that visited Iran in order to make recommendations about: (a) the administrative implications of decentralized planning in Iran; (b) the scope and contents of administration on the regional level; and (c) the establishment of a manpower training center that would be prepared to assume development responsibilities in the regions.

In the course of my visit, I went to some of the most underdeveloped provinces in the nation. In particular, I spent quite a bit of time in Baluchistan, the region in which Ahmed Fazbollah, the peasant I wrote about earlier, lives and farms. I was shocked to see the ways in which the twentieth century had managed to shatter the traditional way of life in this region. The resentment among the peasants was evident to all. Unfortunately, any development project that might have been able to change this situation could not be implemented without the consent and approval of the bureaucracy in Tehran, which, I learned, was vast and corrupt. The governor of Baluchistan, a young and vigorous man with whom I was acquainted, made this clear while showing me plans for a relatively small irrigation scheme, embracing about 2,000 hectares, which had been proposed some three years before by experts in the provincial government. The detailed scheme was based on an intimate knowledge of local conditions and could be implemented at any time. But as the governor of the province explained, the plans had already taken three years to proceed through the "Tehran underground sewage system," namely the bureaucracy, and were still not approved. He said that it would probably take another three years before approval and that then it would cost double what it would have initially: "Half would go for the project, and the other half for the 'guiding hands' of the various intermediaries on the way."

Those were the words of a young man fighting for what he knew was the fate of his country. I asked him whether the Shah knew of this situation. He said that the Shah was surrounded by such a thick wall of ministers, aides, and court officials that it was doubtful he knew how bad things had become. Given what I had learned, it was evident that the royal decree would have little or no effect unless substantial changes were made in the way the government operated on the national level.

On returning to Tehran, I wrote a brief, forthright report, and in informal discussion of my findings with my fellow experts on the UN panel, pulled no punches. Then, at an informal reception for our delegation's final meeting, attended by Iran's minister of economic affairs, I remarked that:

I feel that a very strong earthquake is imminent in this country. There is terrible pressure pent up in every province I visited, mainly due to the widespread knowledge that the capacity for development change and means toward it are available, though nothing along these lines is being implemented in the field. The people know of the existence in Tehran of a luxurious and corrupt organism that is sucking the country dry and wasting the means by which the Iranian people could emerge out of subsistence.

I then added that unless something drastic was done quickly, the ground would indeed quake.

What I said was politely refuted by one of the vice-ministers who informed me that my "Western " way of thinking, my "ignorance" of the Iranian heritage, and my lack of awareness of the fidelity of the Iranian security forces to the Shah's government indicated the preposterous nature of my statement.

The rest is history.

Unless experiences such as Iran's, and Nicaragua's, and Uganda's, and countless others are taken as warnings that effective development at almost any cost is necessary to prevent such revolutions, other developing nations will find themselves facing similar situations. It is time for those in power to realize that relinquishing some power to implement decentralization in support of a regional approach to development, with its greater voice for the masses, is preferable to losing all power.[3]

The age of successful development planning without enfranchisement of the target population in the decisionmaking process has past. In those days, Franco's Spain and Chaing's Taiwan served as examples of economic growth through such measures imposed from above as land reform. Today, as is evident in the broadly based anti-government movements extending from the Philippines to Chile, peasants and workers are armed with knowledge and in many cases weapons.

Although there is still far too much shortsightedness in the developing world today, there are also a number of bright spots where integrated regional planning has been successfully implemented:

The innovations undertaken by Yugoslavia decisively established a new pattern of socialized planning. Although central control over the amount and general direction of investment was retained, many decision-making powers were delegated to nonpolitical authorities under a more or less self-adjusting system of automatic economic controls. These changes gradually eliminated most detailed [Eastern Bloc-style centralized] planning measures and controls over the economy. . . . Socialized enterprises, managed through workers' councils elected by the workers themselves, are permitted to make significant decisions. . . .[4]

The Yugoslavian experiment, in which a mixed economy, with decentralized decisionmaking and other functions, exists under a politically centralized and ideological regime, is one of several examples in which planning and implementation styles similar to those of the Rehovot Centre have produced substantial achievements. To emphasize the point that in order to achieve successful development, those at each level of the society must be involved in decisionmaking, let me quote Seiichi Tobata's comments on Japan in the post-World War II period:

In the past, progress in Japanese agriculture depended on the efforts of the government and of the bureaucracy, sometimes on the landlords, rural merchants, and the processors of agricultural products. Now it is the farmers themselves who have taken over the landlords' role, a fact which augers the beginning of a new rural economic order.[5]

In planning for development, the Japanese also believe in another precept I advocate: the importance of the relationship between economic growth based on a sound agricultural system and the need to retain traditional structures in the society. In this connection, Saburo Okita writes:

I am of the opinion that industrialization is definitely necessary to increase national income and to attain a reasonable rate of economic growth. At the same time I should emphasize the importance of agriculture as the basis for industrialization. Without sound agriculture you cannot provide a domestic market and source of savings to finance industrial development at the initial stage. And without this you cannot succeed in developing industry.

The economic development of a country should be carried out by paying due regard to many traditional factors. It is wrong to regard these factors only as deterrents to economic growth. What is needed in fact is to think out a way by which these factors may be usefully employed . . .[6]

Japan today has joined the ranks of the developed countries. Of course, most developing nations are not starting from the same base postwar Japan had, but that does not mean that Japan's experience should not be remembered. The development planner must look at all the development planning that has been attempted, learning from both success and failure. For example, although China and Japan share many successful development policies, they have very different political regimes and the people they work with have had very different experiences, ways of life, traditions, and education. But if each has been successful in some way, each is worth learning from.

The Chinese experience, which has been much heralded—and deservedly so—for the development innovations it introduced, while similar to Japan's in some ways, is more appropriate in today's world:

In response to the malaise in the countryside and urban-rural income gaps, the Chinese government instituted new policies and revised old ones. . . .

Micro or area specific policies dealing with specific local opportunities and problems . . . are being implemented with a heightened consciousness for economic efficiency particularly at the enterprise level. Along with this is a stress on better economic management, and improved accounting aimed at making state and collectively owned enterprises economic entities responsible for their own losses and profits. Communes have however always been treated as units which must make use of their own resources, production, and surpluses. The new policies have not changed this basic requirement but have rather reinforced it.

Macro policies . . . directed at increasing urban and rural polarization deal chiefly with increasing rural income. Because the great majority of China's population is still in the countryside, this set of policies is therefore broadly conceived and aimed at benefitting most of the population.[7]

The integrated, regional planning program being followed in China, again a program with many elements similar to those developed by the teams at the Rehovot Centre, has begun to result in modernized, sound development. Looking at Asia as a whole, Stohr and Taylor note that:

In Asia, China is an exceptional case. The Chinese peasant has indubitably improved both the qualitative and quantitative aspects of his life style since 1950. Between 1950 and 1976, China clearly experienced long term growth and a marked decrease in inequalities. The other Asian countries, however, are marked with increasing regional and interpersonal disparities and in Thailand, Nepal, and India, there has been relative and absolute impoverishment, especially of rural peoples. . . .[8]

What experience teaches us is that integrated regional planning can work if policymakers believe it is necessary and do everything that needs to be done to implement it.

Let me reiterate and emphasize that the planning methodology proposed here is only a tool to achieve an aim. The aim is the channeling of human efforts so as to create conditions where the welfare and contentment of individuals, by which I mean the ordinary citizen, can be achieved. This can be attained only through a particular relationship between society and the individual. Development planning instructs us on how to establish this relationship in terms of the two components of the development process: economic growth and the safeguarding of values systems.

THE ROAD AHEAD

I reach the end of this book with mixed feelings. I am certain that the suggested new approaches could prove valid and that most of the recommendations can be implemented successfully—and I truly believe that development of all nations is possible. Yet, I have a nagging suspicion that all this may be looked upon as little more than an idealist's dream, detached from reality.

A faith in man's ability to shape his own future underlies all that I have put forth here. But the development process is propelled by unyielding forces, and it changes the character and fate of the peoples of the world. In this book, I have tried to interpret the general rules of this process, as well as suggest ways of influencing its direction, in order to ensure that what results from development is beneficial to all.

The thread of doubt is a reaction to the state of the world today. It seems that man has never lived in a time of such rapid change, unrest, contradiction, and despair. Friction and conflict both between and within nations seem to be increasing; the economic gulf between and within them seems to be expanding. And in addition, man today lives in the shadow of "the bomb," constantly aware of the terrifying weapons that can utterly destroy the world in a matter of seconds. An even more immediate and plausible threat is that posed by famine and hunger, which strikes many parts of the world in a dramatic way, such as is currently the case in Ethiopia. The communications media report these realities to every corner of the globe, broadcasting a message of misery and doom that pervades every village and every streetcorner. Against this background, the message of this book, a "Book of Hope," sounds hollow.

What we must do is keep in mind that there has also been rapid progress over the past few decades. "Weapons" such as agricultural technologies that vastly improve production and medical discoveries that save lives and improve the quality of life have been developed at the same time arsenals of destruction have been created. And political man has also changed, albeit at a much slower pace, over a far longer span of time.

In the traditional era, slavery and servitude were the lot of most people. The Industrial Revolution began a spiral of change: as the economic system increasingly met the material needs of the masses, there was time for education, for questions about the quality of life, and in their wake came a fundamental and far-reaching change. Power has been gradually shifting from a few powerful elite to the masses, and as it has, government for and by the people has been spreading. Not all governments are such, but no government does not know—or at least pay lip service to—the principle that the state is for the people. And this offers hope for the future.

The Second Industrial Revolution, which is just beginning, may be able to solve the problem of the daily struggle for the average man; it has begun to in the developed nations and can, although the road will be slow and painful, for the developing nations. Economic welfare is within reach—Malthusian concepts have not been fulfilled, nor will they ever be.

I believe, especially when looking back at what man has already achieved, that we can determine our future. The remaining question is: Do we want to?

In an ancient Jewish fable the Redeemer of the world sat leperous at the gates of the city, sat and waited, waited silently, patiently, looking at the masses that walked past the gates. A curious person approached him and asked, "For whom are you waiting?" "For you," replied the Redeemer.

PHYSICAL SPATIAL MODEL FOR ECONOMIC GROWTH WITHOUT GEOGRAPHICAL MOBILITY

The material obtained from the country profiles enabled the Rehovot team to determine the sectoral shifts that take place in the various countries studied. Some of the countries examined are developed beyond the primary material needs stage, while others were still in it. The tables represent a three-dimensional model. One dimension denotes economic growth and is subdivided into three stages, namely, that of the primary material needs, social competition, and, finally, the stage of full affluency.

The second dimension is the spatial organization expressed by the level of functions. For this purpose, the local level was subdivided into the village and intervillage rural centers. The regional level is represented by the provincial towns (rural towns) and the main regional towns. The national level is represented by the metropolitan center.

The third dimension describes each of the physical elements needed to fulfill the economic and social needs of the population at each stage and on each level of functions. The physical elements—for instance, primary schools, clinics, community centers, packing houses, agricultural machinery centers, industrial plants, administrative offices, residential dwellings for the population, and so forth—have been categorized by their size, quality, and efficiency by the letters, A, B, and C, which denote improved and enhanced quality, larger scale, and more efficient services, respectively. The characteristics of each element differ from the others according to the economic or social functions they are designed to fulfill.

Table A-1: Physical Spatial Model for Economic
Growth Without Geographical Mobility

| | Level of Functioning | | | | |
| | Local | | Regional | | National |
Function	Village	Inter-Rural Center	Provincial Town	Regional Town	Metropolitan Center
Educational Services					
Kindergarten	A	—	B	At this stage of growth, the regional town fulfills the same function as the provincial town	B
Primary Education	—	A	A		B
Secondary Education	—	—	A		B
Higher Education	—	—	—		A, B
Vocational Training	—	—	A, B		B, C
Health Services					
Clinics, Maternity Services	A	B	B		B, C
General Hospitals	—	—	A, B		B, C
Specialized Hospitals	—	—	—		B
Culture and Entertainment					
Religious Services	X	—	X		X
Community Centers	A	B	B		B, C
Sports Centers	A	B	B		B, C
Entertainment	A	B	B		B, C

Agricultural and Economic Services

	1	2	3	4
Centralization and Packing	—	B	B	—
Marketing and Supply	—	A	A	B
Transport Centers	—	A	B	B
Agricultural Machinery Centers	—	A	B	—

Industry

	1	2	3	4
Processing	—	—	2+1	2
Neutral (footloose) Industries	—	—	1	2
Heavy and Specialized	—	—	—	2+1
Industrial Services	—	—	1	2+1

Administrative Services

	1	2	3	4
Guidance, Experimentation, and Research	—	A+B	B	—
Credit and Investment	—	—	B	C
Administrative Offices	—	—	A	C

Housing of Population

	1	2	3	4
% Farmers	95	2	3	—
% Direct Services to Farmers	20	20	3	10
% Industrial Workers	—	5	35	60
% General Services	5	20	20	55
% Government Services	—	35	—	65

Table A–2: Spatial System and Elements of Planning for the Social Competition Stage

| | Local | | Regional | | National |
| | | | | | |
Function	Village	Inter-Rural Center	Provincial Town	Regional Town	Metropolitan Center
Educational Services					
Kindergarten	B	—	B	C	C
Primary Education	—	B	B	C	C
Secondary Education	—	B	B	C	C
Higher Education	—	—	A	A+B	B+C
Vocational Training	—	—	—	—	—
Health Services					
Clinics, Maternity Services	—	B	B	B+C	B+C
General Hospitals	—	—	B	B, C	B, C
Specialized Hospitals	—	—	—	B	C
Culture and Entertainment					
Religious Services	X	—	X	X	X
Community Centers	—	B	B, C	B, C	B, C
Sports Centers	—	B	B, C	B, C	B, C
Entertainment	B	B, C	B, C	C	C

Agricultural and Economic Services

Centralization and Packing	—	—	B, C	B, C	—
Marketing and Supply	B	B, C	B, C	B, C	C
Transport Centers	—	—	B, C	B, C	C
Agricultural Machinery Centers	B	B	B, C	—	—
Industry					
Processing	—	—	2 + 1	—	—
Neutral (footloose) Industries	—	1	—	2	3
Heavy and Specialized	—	—	—	—	2 + 1
Industrial Services	—	—	1	2 + 1	3 + 2
Administrative Services					
Guidance. Experimentation, and Research	—	B	B	—	—
Credit and Investment	—	—	B	B + C	C
Administrative Offices	—	—	A + B	B + C	C
Housing of Population					
% Farmers	90	5	5	—	—
% Direct Services to Farmers	15	35	35	15	45
% Industrial Workers	5	10	20	20	30
% General Services	10	10	25	25	
% Government Services	2	3	25	30	40

Table A-3: Spatial System and Elements of Physical Planning for Full Affluency

	Level of Functioning				
	Local		Regional		National
Function	Village	Inter-Rural Center	Provincial Town	Regional Town	Metropolitan Center
Educational Services					
Kindergarten	C	—	C	C	C
Primary Education	—	C	C	C	C
Secondary Education	—	C	C	C	C
Higher Education	—	—	A, B	B, C	C
Vocational Training	—	—	—	—	—
Health Services					
Clinics, Maternity Services	—	B	C	C	C
General Hospitals	—	—	B	C	C
Specialized Hospitals	—	—	C	C	C
Culture and Entertainment					
Religious Services	—	—	X	X	X
Community Centers	—	C	C	C	C
Sports Centers	—	C	C	C	C
Entertainment	C	C	C	C	C

Agricultural and Economic Services

Centralization and Packing	—	—	C	C	—
Marketing and Supply	B, C	—	C	C	C
Transport Centers	—	—	B, C	B, C	C
Agricultural Machinery Centers	B, C	—	C	—	—
Industry					
Processing	1	2	3	3	—
Neutral (footloose) Industries	—	2 + 1	2	2	—
Heavy and Specialized	—	1	—	2	3
Industrial Services	—	—	2	3	3
Administrative Services					
Guidance, Experimentation, and Research	—	—	C	C	—
Credit and Investment	—	—	B, C	C	C
Administrative Offices	—	—	B	C	C
Housing of Population					
% Farmers	70	10	10	10	—
% Direct Services to Farmers	20	40	30	30	—
% Industrial Workers	10	15	20	30	25
% General Services	10	10	35	30	15
% Government Services	2	3	35	35	25

DATA FOR THE PRINCIPLE OF OPTIMAL MIX

The tables and figures of this appendix were prepared by Dr. Jacques Silber of the Bar Ilan University Department of Economics (Ramat Gan, Israel). The author gratefully acknowledges Dr. Silber's contribution as an integral part of this study.

Figure B-3 depicts the situation of governments who are interested on one hand by the maximizing the growth rate of the GNP per capita (eventually because this would increase their chances of being reelected), and on the other hand by increasing the intervention of the government (because this increases their power). Using the traditional tools of economic analysis we can draw indifference curves representing the various combination of growth rates and Mix giving a given level of utility to the governments.

But there are constraints which these governments have to face since not every growth rate is compatible with any investment Mix. The curve (C) represents this constraint curve and has a shape similar to the one we observed in our principal analysis. The curve (U) is the curve representing the highest level of utility compatible with the constraint curve. This gives us an optimal position—the point B.

On the contrary if the growth rate was the only objective, its maximal value (and hence the greatest utility level) would correspond to point A, situated to the left of B and corresponding therefore to a lower investment Mix.

Table B–1: Basic Data — Set A Countries

Country	Income per Capita in 1970	Investment Mix (average 60-73) in percent	GNP per Capita Annual Growth Rate Average (1963-1975)
Austria	1,730	20	5.2
Belgium	2,898	15	4.6
Canada	3,367	18	3.6
Denmark	2,898	21	3.8
Finland	1,998	20	5.2
France	2,550	15	5.0
Germany	2,752	16	3.9
Honduras	259	10	1.1
Ireland	1,244	21	3.9
Italy	1,591	12	4.2
Japan	1,636	15	9.6
South Korea	252	26	8.8
Malta	721	31	7.0
The Netherlands	2,232	19	4.4
Norway	2,458	16	3.8
Panama	646	14	4.5
Philippines	225	12	2.8
Portugal	684	15	7.8
South Africa	680	18	2.1
Spain	884	12	5.1
Sweden	3,724	24	2.4
Switzerland	2,963	18	3.2
United Kingdom	1,990	25	2.3
Zambia	345	27	-0.4

Table B-2: Basic Data — Set B Countries

Country	Population in 1970 (thousands)	GDP per Capita (in 1970 $ U.S.)	Investment Mix (%)
Afghanistan	14,300	72	71
Algeria	13,440	332	73
Argentina	23,212	964	34
Bangladesh	70,800	89	82
Barbados	236	661	17
Bolivia	4,931	165	41
Brazil	92,764	393	32
Burma	27,584	78	45
Burundi	3,367	61	8
Cameroon	5,836	177	12
Central Africa	1,601	145	6
Chad	3,640	74	8
Chile	9,720	686	34
Colombia	21,632	320	19
Congo	1,102	269	8
Costa Rica	1,729	508	11
Cyprus	634	852	19
Dominican Republic	4,006	366	29
Ecuador	6,093	305	12

Table B–2: (continued)

Country	Population in 1970 (thousands)	GDP per Capita (in 1970 $ U.S.)	Investment Mix (%)
Egypt	33,329	205	83
El Salvador	3,438	290	11
Ethiopia	24,630	67	17
Fiji	520	377	22
Gabon	493	673	27
Ghana	8,640	230	26
Greece	8,793	1,039	15
Guatemala	4,860	367	12
Guinea	3,920	95	46
Guyana	719	366	43
Honduras	2,509	270	28
Hong Kong	3,959	672	14
Iceland	205	2,283	11
India	538,129	92	37
Indonesia	115,567	60	35
Iran	29,146	383	58
Iraq	9,440	356	39
Ireland	2,944	1,187	47
Israel	2,910	1,801	27
Ivory Coast	5,065	298	33
Jamaica	1,880	673	23

Jordan	2,310	227	50
Kenya	11,220	137	23
Korea	31,435	229	18
Kuwait	750	3,879	43
Lebanon	2,726	542	8
Liberia	1,317	296	27
Libya	1,940	1,874	59
Madagascar	7,067	128	28
Malawi	4,476	67	60
Malaysia	10,877	347	38
Mali	5,050	60	9
Malta	330	673	40
Mauritania	1,160	169	28
Mauritius	835	224	36
Mexico	50,670	613	18
Morocco	15,495	209	42
Nicaragua	2,021	402	16
Niger	4,016	94	20
Nigeria	66,174	97	7
Pakistan	62,640	151	41
Panama	1,434	699	21
Paraguay	2,235	259	34
Peru	13,339	423	32
Philippines	36,852	230	12
Saudi Arabia	7,360	509	96
Senegal	3,830	216	9

Table B–2: (continued)

Country	Population in 1970 (thousands)	GDP per Capita (in 1970 $ U.S.)	Investment Mix (%)
Sierra Leone	2,611	168	21
Singapore	2,075	542	43
Spain	33,645	914	16
Sri Lanka	12,572	93	36
Sudan	15,695	103	18
Syria	6,303	238	75
Tanzania	12,900	94	27
Thailand	35,500	183	19
Togo	1,956	139	9
Trinidad-Tobago	1,027	832	22
Tunisia	5,127	263	42
Turkey	35,230	394	22
Uganda	9,814	117	33
Upper Volta	5,384	64	16
Uruguay	2,886	739	11
Venezuela	10,349	1,067	39
Zaire	18,100	106	26
Zambia	4,264	345	57

Table B–3: Regression Results from the Cross-Section Analysis *

Set A: 24 countries; period 1960-1973; dependent variable = growth rate of the GNP per capita

Exogenous Variables	Regression 1	Regression 2
R^2	0.21	0.30
Constant	-33	-33
MIX	621	644
	(2.2)	(2.2)
$(MIX)^2$	-3245	-3266
	(-2.3)	(-2.2)
$(MIX)^3$	5351	5226
	(2.3)	(2.2)
GNPCAP		-0.0074
		(-1.4)
POPRATE		-0.8
		(-1.2)

* *Note:* GNPCAP = GNP per capita in 1970.
    POPRATE = Population (annual) growth rate.
    t = values in parenthesis.

199

Table B–4: Regression Results from the Cross-Section Analysis *

Set B: 84 countries; period 1965-1973

Exogenous Variables	Regression 1	Regression 2	Regression 3	Regression 4	Regression 5	Regression 6	Regression 7
R^2	0.32	0.37	0.26	0.34	0.23	0.23	0.09
Constant	4.2	-1.4	25.3	-0.07	26.5	26.6	0.86
POPUL	0.0003	0.0003	0.0003	—	$-4E^6$	—	$-7.1E^6$
	(2.0)	(1.9)	(1.7)	—	(-0.08)	—	(-0.1)
$(POPUL)^2$	$-5.7E^{10}$	$-5.5E^{10}$	$-5.5E^{10}$	—	—	—	—
	(-1.9)	(-1.9)	(-1.8)	—	—	—	—
GDPCAP	68.1	58	13.5	55.5	11.6	11.7	6.6
	(5.9)	(4.3)	(2.5)	(4.1)	(2.3)	(2.2)	(1.2)
POPRATE	—	-0.4	-1.2	-0.34	-1.15	-1.15	1
	—	(-1.1)	(-4.0)	(-0.9)	(-3.8)	(-3.8)	1
MIX	—	189	235	202	244	245	290
	—	(1.5)	(1.7)	(1.6)	(1.8)	(1.8)	(2.0)
$(MIX)^2$	—	-525	-624	-556	-648	-646	-824
	—	(-1.6)	(-1.8)	(-1.7)	(-1.8)	(-1.8)	(-2.3)
$(MIX)^3$	—	408	469	433	490	490	634
	—	(1.7)	(1.9)	(1.8)	(1.9)	(1.9)	(2.3)

* *Note:* POPUL = Population size of the country in 1970.
GDPCAP = GDP per capita in 1970.
POPRATE = Population (annual) growth rate.
t = values in parenthesis.

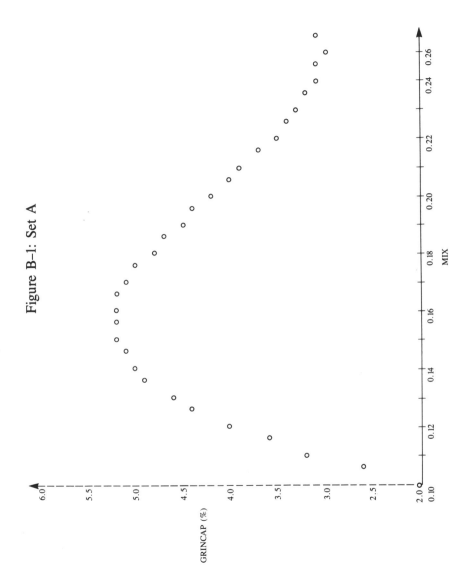

Figure B-1: Set A

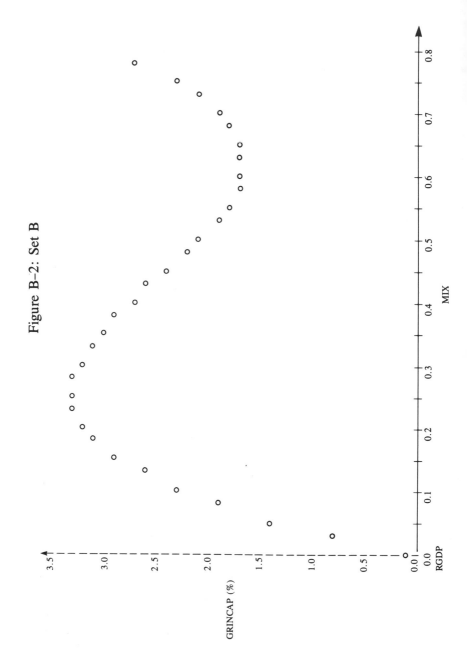

Figure B-2: Set B

Table B–5: Predicted Annual Growth Rate of the GNP per Capita as a Function
of the Population Size, the GNP per Capita, and the Investment Mix

Population = 1 Million Inhabitants

Value of the Mix	GNP per Capita = $100	GNP per Capita = $500	GNP per Capita = $1000	GNP per Capita = $2000
0.5	0.2	2.4	4.2	4.9
0.10	0.8	3.0	4.8	5.4
0.15	1.2	5.4	5.2	5.8
0.20	1.4	3.6	5.4	6.0
0.25	1.5	3.6	5.4	6.1
0.30	1.4	3.6	5.4	6.0
0.35	1.3	3.4	5.2	5.9
0.40	1.1	3.2	5.0	5.7
0.45	0.9	3.0	4.8	5.5
0.50	0.7	2.9	4.7	5.3
0.55	0.6	2.7	4.5	5.2
0.60	0.5	2.7	4.5	5.1

Table B-5: (continued)

Population = 10 Million Inhabitants

Value of the Mix	GNP per Capita = $100	GNP per Capita = $500	GNP per Capita = $1000	GNP per Capita = $2000
0.5	0.5	2.7	4.5	5.1
0.10	1.1	3.2	5.0	5.7
0.15	1.5	3.6	5.4	6.1
0.20	1.7	3.8	5.6	6.3
0.25	1.7	3.9	5.7	6.3
0.30	1.7	3.8	5.6	6.3
0.35	1.5	3.7	5.5	6.1
0.40	1.3	3.5	5.3	5.9
0.45	1.1	3.3	5.1	5.7
0.50	0.9	3.1	4.9	5.5
0.55	0.8	3.0	4.8	5.4
0.60	0.8	2.9	4.7	5.4

Population = 50 Million Inhabitants

Value of the Mix	GNP per Capita = $100	GNP per Capita = $500	GNP per Capita = $1000	GNP per Capita = $2000
0.5	1.5	3.7	5.5	6.1
0.10	2.1	4.2	6.0	6.7
0.15	2.4	4.6	6.4	7.0
0.20	2.6	4.8	6.6	7.2
0.25	2.7	4.9	6.7	7.3
0.30	2.6	4.8	6.6	7.2
0.35	2.5	4.7	6.5	7.1
0.40	2.3	4.5	6.3	6.9
0.45	2.1	4.3	6.1	6.7
0.50	1.9	4.1	5.9	6.5
0.55	1.8	4.0	5.8	6.4
0.60	1.7	3.9	5.7	6.3

Table B-5: (continued)

Population = 100 Million Inhabitants

Value of the Mix	GNP per Capita = $100	GNP per Capita = $500	GNP per Capita = $1000	GNP per Capita = $2000
0.5	2.5	4.7	6.5	7.1
0.10	3.1	5.2	7.0	7.7
0.15	3.5	5.6	7.4	8.1
0.20	3.7	5.8	7.6	8.3
0.25	3.7	5.9	7.7	8.3
0.30	3.7	5.8	7.6	8.1
0.35	3.5	5.7	7.5	7.9
0.40	3.3	5.5	7.3	7.7
0.45	3.1	5.3	7.1	7.5
0.50	2.9	5.1	6.9	7.4
0.55	2.8	5.0	6.8	7.4
0.60	2.8	4.9	6.7	7.4

Population = 500 Million Inhabitants

Value of the Mix	GNP per Capita = $100	GNP per Capita = $500	GNP per Capita = $1000	GNP per Capita = $2000
0.3	1.3	3.5	5.3	5.9
0.10	1.9	4.0	5.8	6.5
0.15	2.3	4.4	6.2	6.9
0.20	2.5	4.6	6.4	7.1
0.25	2.5	4.7	6.5	7.1
0.30	2.5	4.6	6.4	7.0
0.35	2.3	4.5	6.3	6.9
0.40	2.1	4.3	6.1	6.7
0.45	1.9	4.1	5.9	6.5
0.50	1.7	3.9	5.7	6.3
0.55	1.6	3.8	5.6	6.2
0.60	1.6	3.7	5.5	6.2

Figure B-3: Optimal Mix Constraints and Objective Function

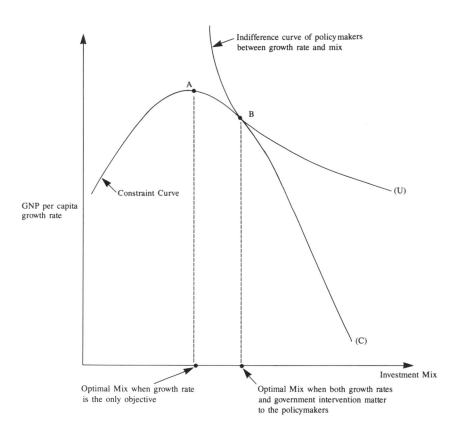

208

Table B-6: Regression Results from the Time-Series Analysis *

United Kingdom (1959-1977)—Range of the Mix: 0.37-0.51; Dependent Variable = Logarithm of the GNP per Capita (GDPCAP)

Exogenous Variables	Regression 1	Regression 2	Regression 3	Regression 4
R^2	0.007	0.98	0.98	0.98
Constraint	0.05	-19.3	-19.2	-24.1
ln POPUL	—	-1.79	1.78	1.8
		(2.1)	(1.96)	(2.0)
MIX	-0.085	-0.15	0.04	27.9
	(-0.33)	(-0.72)	(0.013)	(0.5)
$(MIX)^2$	—	—	-0.21	-63.8
			(-0.06)	(-0.5)
$(MIX)^3$	—	—	—	48.0
				(0.5)
TIME	—	0.014	0.014	0.014
		(3.8)	(3.45)	(3.3)
D.W.	2.5	1.99	1.99	2.0
δ	0.94	-0.01	-0.01	-0.03

* *Note:* TIME = Vector equal to 1959, . . . 1977.

D.W. = Durbin Watson Statistics.

δ = Autocorrelation coefficient of the disturbances.

ln = natural logarithm.

t = values in parenthesis.

209

Table B-7: Regression Results from the Time-Series Analysis *

France (1959-1978)—Range of the Mix: 0.13–0.18; Dependent Variable = Logarithm of the GDP per Capita (GDPCAP)

Exogenous Variables	Regression 1	Regression 2	Regression 3
R^2	0.65	0.93	0.96
Constant	0.43	0.91	2.03
ln (POPUL)	—	0.11 (0.50)	—
POPUL	—	—	U. SE[6] (1.01)
(MIX)	-1.15 (-5.6)	-9.3 (-3.16)	— (-2.0)
(MIX)^2	—	26.0 (2.7)	749 (2.0)
(MIX)^3	—	—	-1562 (-1.9)
TIME	—	0.023 (7.7)	0.026 (10.8)
δ	0.96	0.90	0.87
D.W.	2.5	2.5	2.5

* *Note*: POPUL = Population size of the country in 1970.
    TIME = Vector equal to 1959, . . . 1978.
    δ = Autocorrelation coefficient of the disturbances.
    D.W. = Durbin Watson Statistics.
    ln = natural logarithm.
    t = values in parenthesis.

It can be seen that the value of MIX for which ln (GDPCAP) is equal to zero, is 0.18, (using the results of Regression 2). Since ln (GDPCAP) = -9.3 + 26 (MIX), the rate of growth of GDPCAP first increases, then decreases with MIX.

Table B-8: Regression Results from the Time-Series Analysis *

Israel (1962-1977)—Range of the Mix: 32%-48%; Dependent Variable = ln (GNPCAP)

Exogenous Variables	Regression 1	Regression 2
R²	0.94	0.95
Constant	-26	-25
ln (POPUL)	6.45	6.5
	(3.5)	(3.6)
(MIX)	0.055	-0.34
	(1.7)	(-0.7)
(MIX)²	-0.0007	0.009
	(1.9)	(-0.7)
(MIX)³	—	-0.00009
	—	(-0.8)
TIME	-0.15	-0.15
	(-2.0)	(-2.8)
D.W.	2.11	1.94
δ	0.47	0.44

* *Note:* ln (POPUL) = TK.
TIME = Vector equal to 1959, . . . 1977.
D.W. = Durbin Watson Statistics.
δ = Autocorrelation coefficient of the disturbances.
t = values in parentheses.
ln = natural logarithm.

It can be shown using Regression 1 that the values of MIX which maximizes ln (GNPCAP) is equal to 37%.

Table B-9: Regression Results from the Time-Series Analysis *

Greece (1949-1977)—Range of the Mix: 0.22-0.35; Dependent Variable: ln (GDPCAP)

Exogenous Variables	Regression 1	Regression 2	Regression 3
R^2	0.06	0.30	0.55
Constant	0.057	0.056	1.36
POPUL	—	—	0.00026
			(-1.4)
TIME	—	—	(7.3)
(MIX)	0.24	6.24	8.7
	(-2.1)	(2.2)	(2.8)
(MIX)^2	—	-17.3	-23.7
		(-2.2)	(-2.7)
(MIX)^3	—	14.6	19.9
		(2.2)	(2.6)
δ	1	1	0.55
D.W.	2.2	1.7	1.8

* *Note:* TIME = Vector equal to 1959, . . 1978.
  δ = Autocorrelation coefficient of the disturbances.
  D.W. = Durbin Watson Statistics.
  ln = natural logarithm.
  t = values in parenthesis.

See Figure B-4 for critical values of MIX.

Figure B-4: Critical Values of MIX

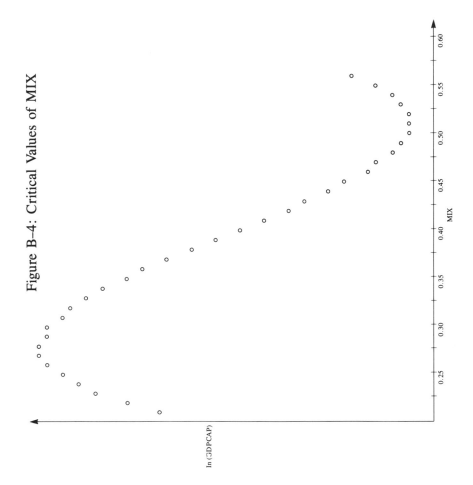

A PRACTICAL GUIDE FOR THE SOCIAL PLANNER

The following table summarizes the roles assumed by the social planner operating as part of the planning team according to the Development Frame of Reference.

Assuring Basic Needs	Social Competition	Full Affluency
Local Level: Production Cells		
1. Introduction and infiltration of worthwhile development methods	1. Coordination of types of agricultural specialization to nature of family	1. Planning of economic operations is carried out by the private sector (the state planning system provides only data and guidance)
2. Coordination of new branches, suited to structure and tendency of family	2. Guidance in choice of service and industrial professions to the non-agricultural second generation	2. Family guidance (study and training, leisure, human relations, intergenerational relations)
3. Coordination of vocational training with services and industry	3. Determination of the elements of the motivational system in accordance with the specialization process	
4. Motivation on the individual level	4. Family planning	
5. Family planning (nutrition, children, health, labor organization)		
Local Level: Rural and Urban Communities		
1. Guidance in determining community organization (cooperative, collective, combined farm, administered farm)	As in previous stage	1. Determination of social frameworks for "integrated" rural communities

216

2. Methods for suggesting importance of community organization (information, sampling, leadership mobility, political influence)

3. Guidance in physical planning of rural community

4. Guidance in planning new urban neighborhoods

Regional Level

1. Demographic calculations and forecasts

2. Coordination of regional plans to nature and tendencies of population

3. Guidance in planning of economic and civilian services (location, size administration, institutions)

2. Determination of civil-service standards according to the structure of the rural community

3. Direction of treatment for welfare cases and delinquents

4. Determination of expectations of economic growth and the value systems

5. Family guidance

1. Regional demographic calculations and forecasts

2. Choice of regional specialization and direction of production procedures in the three sectors

3. Guidance in planning of economic and civilian services

1. Planning of medium-sized industries specific to the regions

2. Planning of regional-level service installations

3. Methods of data collection and transfer to national level

Assuring Basic Needs	Social Competition	Full Affluency
4. Analysis of food basket and its coordination with agricultural development plan and habits of population	4. Guidance in extending urban foci and planning central urban neighborhoods	
5. Rules for choosing new settlers for new settlements	5. Rules for organizing regional development tools	
6. Planning and implementing regional information system	6. Social research and surveys	
7. Research surveys in social field		
8. Guidance in housing construction and environmental planning		

National Level

Assuring Basic Needs	Social Competition	Full Affluency
1. National demographic calculations and forecasts	1. National demography	1. National demography
2. Determination of strategy for interregional and geographic mobility	2. Guidance for determination of regional preferences	2. Determination of regional preferences

3. Social projections of objectives and distribution of national resources for development goals (distribution of incomes)

4. Guidance on implementation of national information system

5. Institutional structure of development bodies

3. Determination of national norms for service systems

4. Research and survey center for social problems in development process

5. Guidance for determination of strategy of spatial settlement, especially metropoli

3. Determination of norms for welfare policies

4. Social planning, guidance of metropolitan areas

5. Participation in plan at request of instructors

6. National leisure program

7. Research center in social and development problems

Our suggested model for social development planning enumerates five levels of function, rather than the usual four, because two types of social functioning are distinguished at the local level—that of the individual and his family, and that of the rural and urban communities. It is also pointed out that although the grid describes the functions of the planner, it is in fact based on a number of fundamental assumptions drawn from the concept and content of social planning and its function in achieving a social order appropriate to the economic conditions at each stage of growth.

The Level of the Individual. In the preliminary stages of economic growth, social planning should be entrusted to government machinery as an integral part of their development plans. At this stage, and particularly during the transition from the first to the second stage, the social planner has three main functions:

1. Coordinating suggested improvements in production, in general, and in agriculture, in particular, with the structure, interest, and ability of the average family within the target population. Coordinating crops with the type of population in each region is extremely important, because changes in the economic structure will be successful only if exploitation of the basic means of agricultural production is in tune with the character and inclination of the labor force. The labor force is the main factor to be fully and efficiently exploited at the critical stage of transition from subsistence to mixed farming. The social planner's role in the planning team at this stage is one of the pre-conditions for the success of the development project.

2. Explaining to both manufacturers and the population at large how the overall development plan will affect local conditions. At this stage, an understanding of the sphere of the development plan should more or less disperse the day-to-day economic worries of the small agricultural manufacturers and the general population and should defuse social pressures. The changes in agricultural production suggested by the planning team should not only advance the overall plan but also be relevant and comprehensible to the farmers themselves. The social planner should closely study the nature and tendencies of the population and then determine the principles and frameworks for disseminating information in the right way. He must coordinate professional training for service workers and particularly for industrial workers who will soon enter the regional areas. The younger generation, which will not be absorbed into agriculture, must be trained and prepared to fill roles outside the traditional framework. This part of the program, too, must be formulated in light of local conditions.

3. "Family planning." This must be viewed in a wider sense than just planning the number of children. The economic growth process affects

change in the traditional nutrition, housing, and clothing of the population, and a different way of life results. The social planner must predict these changes and define, analyze, and explain them in a series of informative, standard, and organizational operations, so that the changes which result from economic growth, and which are an inseparable part of the overall development process, will take place as the plan is implemented.

Throughout, the social planner must function as a member of the planning team. He must participate in analyzing operative plans, learn from other team members about the aims and pressures under which the program is being implemented, and modify elements within the comprehensive framework according to professional expertise. At the implementation stage, he must take part in, influence, and be influenced by all aspects of the process. This is true not only for the production cell stage (that is, the level of the individual and the family), but for all other stages, too. We shall see that this integration of social planning with general planning differs in strength and intensity at different levels and stages of economic growth.

At the social-competition stage and particularly at the full-affluency stage, this role is returned to government officials and is implemented by the individuals themselves, according to their own understanding and choice. At these levels the advice of experts in social planning will be available on request.

The Community Level. One of the most important functions of the social planner at the onset of the basic-needs stage of economic growth is choosing organizational frameworks for the rural community. We have seen in chapter 4 that the transition from traditional subsistence farming to agriculture for the market involves not only changes in the farm itself but also in the external supporting structure. The first link in this chain is the village itself—that is, the rural community. Individual farmers must unite in appropriate frameworks to make production more efficient, to cooperate in operations of a minimal economic size, and to block the traders who are the parasites of the traditional community and present a major obstacle to the development and growth of the agricultural sector.

There are many different types of community organizations—from the full collective (in which all means of production belong to the community rather than to the family) to the various community cooperatives (in which the single family producer is helped to become more efficient, market his produce, and obtain the necessary credit—the moshav, cooperative unions, producers' cooperatives on the community level—and in which services are run by individuals, each responsible for a section of service and production in the village). The choice of the most suitable and efficient form of community organization naturally arises from the overall policies of the government. We are convinced that each particular situation demands a certain type of community organization, based on existing economic and social factors. The social planner must study the fundamental situation to determine the principles and rules that will steer the policy planners in choosing the type of community organization most suited to the local way of life.

Alongside community organization in the rural villages, the planning of provincial towns must be studied. Urbanization serves as the starting point of development planning at a particular stage and involves basic social changes that require study, clarification, and resolution. The development of provincial towns into homogeneous urban communities is, in our opinion, one of the most efficient ways of developing urban growth centers in agricultural regions. Urbanization becomes especially important in the change-over from the traditional to the basic-needs stage. It is also the task of the social planner to determine directives and frameworks for planning units, community-service installations, and social-assistance procedures— all from the perspective of social functioning under economic pressure.

The social planner participates fully in the planning process and, in addition, must determine rules and principles for the implementation of the development plan. He must suggest ways in which the changes dictated by the economic plan can be introduced into the rural and urban community organizations. To explain the development plan and convince the target population that it is socially viable, the social planner will use polls and information techniques, mobilize local authorities, and work with local and national political bodies.

Social planning on the community level is subject to the state authorities responsible for implementing the planned and indirectly instigated operations during the first two stages. At the preliminary stages, the need for intervention is greater. As a society experiences economic growth, living, educational, and vocational training standards rise, and there is greater social and occupational mobility—especially when traditions, reinforced by ramified families and groups, disappear. At the same time, government intervention in the social planning of community organizations is needed less and less. Once a society reaches the social-competition stage and particularly during transition from social competition to full affluency, the rural and urban communities alike can function simply with the assistance of independent economic and physical planning experts. This difference is significant for the task of social planning at these stages.

The Regional Level. It has already been stressed that in the initial stages the center of development operations, in general, and directed operations, in particular, is at the intermediate (regional) level. The main production factor at the beginning is human labor. The importance of allocating the labor force to the three economic sectors in such a way that each sector will develop not only for itself but for the others should therefore be clear. Thus the importance of the regional level at the traditional and basic-needs stages of national development is not only economic, but also social.

At the initial stages of economic growth, there are regional-level social-planning centers in four main areas:

1. Demographic and regional calculations and predictions. This is more than a technical-assistance role based simply on statistics and demographic calculations. The social processes within the local population must also be taken into account to enable realistic forecasts of the result of "family planning" and an understanding of the anticipated outcome of implementing the development plans in the medium and long range. Social planning is therefore responsible for the demographic sector of the entire plan.

2. Integration of a macro-regional plan suited to the populations of both the towns and the villages.

3. Determination of "social" rules for practical and relevant planning of civilian and economic services (educational, cultural, health, marketing, supply, credit, training, research experiments). Practical planning of services will strengthen weak points of development at various stages and require the close cooperation of all members of the planning team to find the appropriate solutions. The team must recommend the size, location, organization, and hierarchy of the various services. Each factor is linked with the agricultural aspects, and each requires directed and professional social analysis.

4. Planning implementation—that is, informing the local population of regional development plans and guiding the penetration of plans into the lives of the people. The methods used at the community level for disseminating the development plan become even more important at the regional level. The important distinction between coercion and explanation and persuasion is the key to understanding the importance of social planning. Training government workers involved in development and, more importantly, the members of the planning team itself, is the task of the social planner. He is also responsible for establishing appropriate relations between those responsible for implementation and the target population—that is, between the operators and those "operated on."

At the social-competition stage and during transition to full affluency, the center of development operations moves steadily from the regional to the national level, as already seen in economic planning. With the maturing of the social-competition stage, its accompanying features of specialized production (production level and income; improvements in services and infrastructure, including transportation and communications; techniques of large-scale data collection and computer analysis; homogenization of society) all move to the national level, and the regional level serves only for data collection, sorting and transfer. Development planning units are concentrated in the nerve center of the state and from there operate the economic tools at their disposal. The social planner works from the same center as an integral part of the planning team.

The National Level. At the initial stages of development, social planning on the national level is chiefly concerned with guiding policy rather than being integrated into the planning process itself. Social aspects have a defined significance and importance for economic-growth policy, and the function of the social planner is to collect data and accumulate enough information so that the policymakers can determine policies. At this stage, the main functions of social planning are:

1. National demographic calculations and forecasts. As these are the basis on which a wide range of policies are determined, they should be a summary of demographic calculations in each region. At this stage, all national demographic data and forecasts should be based on work in those regions with which the social planners are in direct contact—otherwise national demography will be more guesswork than a collection of real data.

2. Creation of a social background against which geographic-mobility strategy and preferences among the regions can be determined. This background is also required for national-level economic and spatial planning in which social aspects determine preferences for the distribution of resources among the various regions. Most important of all, it is required for directing the growth of the large towns, especially the metropoli.

3. Systems of information and national guidance (indoctrination)—a special and very responsible task undertaken by the social planner in the preliminary stages. The influence of social aspects on information systems is great and unique. The systems must take into account the way of life and ethnic and cultural composition of many diverse groups and create a social mosaic within the national network.

In conclusion, two separate, though integrated, tasks are the province of the social planner. The first is to use social factors to assist economic growth and to strengthen the social order through ideologies derived from the social-values system. The second is to help develop the basic-values system, which, by equipping the individual from birth with a firm emotional foundation, protects him from the most dangerous of his enemies—nihilism and the denial of himself and his purpose in life.

The social planner's task falls into four stages, and his/her approach changes at each stage: (a) when the planning team is set up; (b) when the program is arranged; (c) when the program is publicized; and (d) when the program is implemented.

In the first stage the planner behaves as a sociologist, seeking information about the social, authoritative, and political systems, and attempts to analyze and forecast the initial responses of the target population. In the second stage the planner, no longer a lone social investigator, joins with the team in translating theory into planning principles and drawing up operative plans. In the third stage the planner returns to the field and functions as an administrator examining planning at a practical level. His task now is to see whether plans are successful, whether the expectations and demands of the population are being met, whether the authoritative institutional system is coordinated with the development plans, and whether the plans are sufficiently flexible. And in the fourth, most important and extended stage of social planning, the social planner works alongside the target population, participating in the development efforts and judging the outcome of the overall plan.

At the first stage the social planner must participate in identifying and locating the target population. He must get to know the parties involved, both the population whom the program will serve, and the policymakers— the government institutions. The planner must learn the positions of all government, political, and representative groups, both those who will work with the planning team and those who will oppose it. By getting to know the parties involved, the planning team can comprehend the social problems involved and how they will affect economic and environmental planning. The social problem is always the major difficulty.

The second stage is the drawing up of plans, and the social planner works with the planning team. The multi-disciplinary team begins by determining alternatives for future operations, and the social planner's function is to bring to the attention of the team the primary responses that he sees arising at each stage. He makes the team aware of the social phenomena identified in stage one and defines the problems to be solved. He also brings before the team the existing authoritative structures—local, regional, and national—as well as the opposing and cooperating social groups, both represented and unrepresented, so that orders of social preference may be established.

The third stage is publicizing the refined program. Once possible alternatives are proposed, the importance of the social planner's role grows. The development plan serves as a type of response mechanism to certain social situations, and speed or delay in reacting to all or part of it will result in public approval or disapproval. The social planner must measure public response to development plans in the primary stages. There are three stages of public participation:

1. Passive participation when the plan is announced. The planner must measure response to the development plan to verify the forecasts he made at stage one.

2. Dialogue with the groups and institutions influencing development and being influenced by it. The social planner must identify the parties and formulate participation techniques—styles of response and dissemination of information to the wider population—and create a primary nucleus of "development leaders." This leads to the third stage.

3. Appropriate participation, in which the involvement of the target population is the most active and positive. The social planner must also set up "response mechanisms," operate them, and remain aware that they will lead to demand for increased participation.

The fourth stage is perhaps the most important. It is determining whether the ambitions, expectations and demands of the target population are both fulfilled and perceived as fulfilled. At this stage the planner returns to the field to work alongside the target population during implementation of the plan.

NOTES

CHAPTER 1

1. W. W. Leontief, "The Distribution of Work and Income," *Scientific American* 247, 3 (September 1982).

2. World Bank, *World Development Report, 1980* (Washington, D.C.: World Bank, 1980), pp. 1-2.

3. Ibid., p. 33.

4. Ibid., see Table 1, "Basic Indicators," pp. 110-11.

5. World Bank, *Questions and Answers* (Washington, D.C.: World Bank, 1976).

6. E. S. Mason and R. E. Asher, *The World Bank Since Bretton Woods* (Washington, D.C.: Brookings Institution, 1973), pp. 1-2.

7. L. Pearson, *Partners in Development, Report of the Commission on International Development* (New York: Praeger, 1968), p. 7.

8. United Nations Department of Public Information, *Basic Facts about the United Nations, Summary of Its Purposes, Structures and Activities* (New York: United Nations, 1976).

9. Pearson, *Partners in Development*, p. 30.

10. World Bank, *Questions and Answers*, p. 15.

11. W. Brandt, *North-South: A Program for Survival* (London: Pan Books, 1980).

12. Ibid., p. 290.

13. K. Minogue, "Between Rhetoric and Fantasy," *Encounter* (December 1980).

14. P. D. Henderson, "Economics Askew," in ibid.

15. Gunnar Myrdal, *Asian Drama: An Inquiry into the Poverty of Nations* (New York: Pantheon, 1968).

16. E. M. Rogers, *Modernization Among Peasants—The Impact of Communication* (New York: Holt, Rinehart and Winston, 1969).

17. M. P. Todaro, *Economic Development in the Third World* (London: Longman, 1977), p. 6.

18. N. Jacobs, *Modernization with Development: Thailand as an Asian Case Study* (New York: Praeger, 1971), p. 9.

19. E. E. Hagen, quoted in G. Myrdal, *Asian Drama*, 3, p. 1972.

20. G. Dalton, *Economic Systems and Society* (Harmondsworth, United Kingdom: Penguin Books, 1974).

21. Albert Waterson, *Development Planning: Lessons of Experience* (Baltimore, Md.: Johns Hopkins University Press, 1965), p. 170.

22. W. W. Kohler, *The Place of Value in a World of Facts* (New York: Liveright, 1938).

23. J. Winnie and W. W. William, *Latin American Development* (Los Angeles: University of California Press, 1967); E. B. Ayal, "Value Systems and Economic Development in Japan and Thailand," *Journal of Social Issues* 19, 1 (January 1963), pp. 35-51.

24. For example, J. Kahl in *The Measurement of Modernism* (Austin: University of Texas Press, 1969), p. 6 states:

Traditional values . . . call for fatalistic acceptance of the world as it is, respect for those in authority, and submergence of the individual in the collectivity. Modern values are rational and secular, permit choice and experiment, glorify efficiency and change, and stress individual responsibility.

25. Adam Smith, *The Wealth of Nations* (New York: Random, 1937), p. 28.

26. A. Marshall, *Principles of Economics* (London: Macmillan, 1920), p. 61

27. M. Friedman, *Essays in Positive Economics* (Chicago: University of Chicago Press, 1966).

28. R. T. Herford, trans., *Pirke Abot: The Ethics of the Talmud, Sayings of the Fathers* (New York: Schocken Books, 1962).

CHAPTER 2

1. T. Schultz, *Transforming Traditional Agriculture* (New Haven, Conn.: Yale University Press, 1964).

2. Reported to the author, with special reference to China, at a seminar dealing with problems of rural development (Nagoya, Japan, December 1981).

3. Robert Heilbroner, *The Great Ascent* (New York: Harper and Row, 1963).

4. Alvin Toffler, *The Third Wave* (New York: Bantam Books, 1980), p. 10.

5. Akin L. Mabogunje, "Urbanization in Africa" (Paper delivered at

the Sixth Rehovot (Israel) Conference on Urbanization and Development in Developing Countries, 1971), published in *Conference Papers,* Sixth Rehovot Conference (Rehovot, Israel: Settlement Study Centre, 1971).

6. See F. Dovring, "The Share of Agriculture in a Growing Population," *FAO Monthly Bulletin of Agricultural Economics and Statistics* I-II, (August-September 1950); and Daniel Freeman, "The Transfer of Investment Capital from Developed to Developing Countries," *The Economic Quarterly,* 112 (February 1982), and *The Developing Countries Growth and Monetary Assistance from the Developed and OPEC Countries* (Rehovot, Israel: Settlement Study Centre, 1981).

7. For a fuller description of this case study see Raanan Weitz and Levia Applebaum, "Planning for Full Employment in Rural Areas," prepared for a Ford Foundation Seminar on Rural Development and Employment, Ibadan, Nigeria, April 9-12, 1973. A copy of this paper can be obtained from the Settlement Study Centre, Rehovot, Israel.

8. See Kingsley Davis, "The Role of Urbanization in the Development Process" (Paper prepared for the Sixth Rehovot (Israel) Conference on Urbanization and Development in Developing Countries, 1971); published in *Conference Papers* (Rehovot, Israel: Settlement Study Centre, 1971).

9. Antoni Kuklinski and R. Petrella, eds., *Growth Poles and Regional Policies: A Seminar* (The Hague: Mouton & Co., 1972), p. 1.

10. See Robert J. Crooks, "Urbanization and Social Change: Transitional Urban Settlements in Developing Countries," Robert Sadove, "A Response to the Urban Needs of Developing Countries," and Marshall Clinard, "The Absorption Problems of In-Migration," (Papers delivered at the Sixth Rehovot (Israel) Conference on Urbanization and Development in Developing Countries, 1971), published in *Conference Papers,* Sixth Rehovot Conference (Rehovot, Israel: Settlement Study Centre, 1971).

11. As quoted in Raanan Weitz, ed., *Urbanization and the Developing Countries: Report on the Sixth Rehovot Conference* (New York: Praeger, 1973), p. 14.

12. T. G. McGee, *The Urbanization Process in the Third World* (London: G. Bell, 1971), p. 31.

13. E. Brutzkus, "Centralized versus Decentralized Patterns of Urbanization in Developing Countries: An Attempt to Elucidate a Guideline Principle," *Economic Development and Cultural Change* 23, 4 (July 1975), pp. 633-52.

14. H. Stretton, *Urban Planning in Rich and Poor Countries* (Oxford: Oxford University Press, 1978), p. 104.

15. J. Connell et al., *Migration from Rural Areas* (Delhi: Oxford University Press, 1976).

16. H. Clout, "Rural-Urban Migration in Western Europe," in *Geographical Essay*, ed. J. Salt and H. Clout (London: Oxford University Press, 1976), pp. 30-51.

17. See Connell et al., *Migration from Rural Areas.* For example, formerly patriarchal societies became matriarchal within an exceedingly brief time span.

18. Edmundo Flores, "Economic Growth and Urbanization" (Paper delivered at the Sixth Rehovot (Israel) Conference on Urbanization and Development in Developing Countries, 1971), published in *Conference Papers*, Sixth Rehovot Conference (Rehovot, Israel: Settlement Study Centre, 1971).

19. J. Kahl in *The Measurement of Modernism* (Austin: University of Texas Press, 1969).

20. W. Brandt, *North-South: A Program for Survival* (London: Pan Books, 1980), p. 48.

21. Felipe Herrera, "Nationalism and Urbanization in Latin America" (Paper delivered at the Sixth Rehovot (Israel) Conference on Urbanization and Development in Developing Countries, 1971), published in *Conference Papers,* Sixth Rehovot Conference (Rehovot, Israel: Settlement Study Centre, 1971).

CHAPTER 3

1. Lowdon Wingo, "National Development Objectives and Metropolitan Concentration" (Paper prepared for the Sixth Rehovot, Israel, Conference on Urbanization and Development in Developing Countries, August 1971), published in *Conference Papers* (Rehovot, Israel: Settlement Study Centre, 1971).

2. S. M. Kuznets, *Economic Growth of Nations: Total Output and Production Structure* (Cambridge, Mass.: Belknap Press, 1971).

3. Chenery and Syrquin later extended Kuznets's thesis to developing countries. H. B. Chenery and M. Syrquin, *Patterns of Development, 1950-1970* (London: Oxford University Press, 1975).

4. I. Adelman and C. Morris, *Society, Politics, and Economic Development—Quantitative Approach* (Baltimore, Md.: Johns Hopkins University Press, 1975).

5. H. H. Hyman, *Inducing Social Change in Developing Communities* (Geneva: UNRISD, 1966). Also, UNRISD, *Contents and Measurements of Socioeconomic Development* (New York: Praeger, 1972).

6. M. D. Morris, "A Physical Quality of Life Index (PQLI)," in *The United States and World Development, Agenda, 1976* (New York: Praeger, 1976), pp. 147-71.

7. N. Hicks and P. Streeten, "Indicators of Development: The Search for Basic Needs Yardstick," *World Development* 7 (1979), pp. 567-80.

8. A. B. Atkinson, "On the Measurement of Inequality," *Journal of Economic Theory* 2, 2 (1970).

9. S. Ch. Kolm, "Unequal Inequalities," *Journal of Economic Theory* 12, 3 (1976), pp. 416-42.

10. Morgan D. Thomas, "Growth Pole Theory: An Examination of Some of Its Basic Concepts," in *Growth Center and Regional Economic Development,* ed. Morgan D. Thomas and Miles Hansen (New York: Free Press, 1972).

11. *The Element of Space in Development Planning* (Amsterdam: North-Holland Publishing Company, 1969), p. 1.

12. Tormod Hermansen states in this connection that:

development is to be considered as a unified dynamic temporal process with strong linkages through time . . . any study of development requires a dynamic frame of reference . . . development takes place in a definite spatial setting involving spatial interdependencies (both of simultaneous and inter-temporal character) and has therefore to be analyzed within a spatial-temporal framework.

Tormod Hermansen, "Development Poles and Development," in *Growth Poles and Growth Centres in Regional Planning,* ed. Antoni Kuklinski (The Hague: Mouton and Co., 1972), p. 8. Hermansen credits John Friedmann, especially in his *Regional Development Theory: A Case Study of Venezuela,* as having stressed this point of view.

13. Angel T. Rodriguez et al., *Proyecto de Asentamiento Campesino "El Sisal" (Azua)* (Santo Domingo: Instituto Agrario Dominicano, 1969).

14. Nathaniel Lichtfield, "Economic Growth and Urbanization" (Paper prepared for the Sixth Rehovot Conference), published in *Conference Papers.*

15. David Tanne, "Policies of Rapid Urbanization in Israel" (Paper prepared for the Sixth Rehovot Conference), published in *Conference Papers.*

16. See Chung-Tong and Ip who discuss a regional approach that is being followed in the development program adopted for China's Guandong and Shandong provinces. This program is geared toward "catching up" with the "national" (i.e., metropolitan) standards. Wu Chung-Tong and David F. Ip, *Rural Development and Regional Autonomy in China: Recent Directions in Guangdong and Shandong* (Nagoya, Japan: United Nations Centre for Regional Development, 1981).

17. William Alonso, "Planning and the Spatial Organization of the Metropolis in the Developing Countries" (Paper prepared for the Sixth Rehovot Conference), published in *Conference Papers.*

18. Rodriguez et al., *Proyecto de Asentamiento Campesino "El-Sisal"* *(Azua)*.

19. Yilmaz Gurer, as quoted in Raanan Weitz, ed., *Urbanization and the Developing Countries: Report on the Sixth Rehovot Conference* (New York: Praeger, 1973), p. 121.

20. Moshe Z. Prives, *Bas Boen, A Project of International Cooperation in Agricultural Development in a Hard-Core Poverty Area, Valley of Cul-de-Sac, Haiti* (Rehovot, Israel: Centre for International Agricultural Cooperation, Ministry of Agriculture, 1978), p. 58.

21. Moshe Z. Prives, "A Project in Zambia: Integrated Area Settlement in the Copperbelt" (Mimeo, Centre for International Agricultural Cooperation, Ministry of Agriculture, Rehovot, Israel, 1974).

22. David Pelley, *Planning Process: Nykuru-Nyandarua Region—Kenya* (Rehovot, Israel: Settlement Study Centre, 1982), p. 20.

23. Raanan Weitz, "The Transformation of Ceylonese Peasant Agriculture" (Report submitted for the Organization for Economic Cooperation and Development, Seminar on Development Strategy and Administration, Colombo, Ceylon, 1966). A copy of the paper is available from the Settlement Study Centre, Rehovot, Israel.

24. Prives, "Project in Zambia."

25. See Weitz, "Transformation of Ceylonese Peasant Agriculture," pp. 7, 11.

CHAPTER 4

1. This tendency has become institutionalized in leading studies of development issues. For example, Albert Waterson's study for the World Bank addresses only those issues relating to physical infrastructure and economic enterprises. Albert Waterson, *Development Planning* (Baltimore, Md.: Johns Hopkins University Press, 1963).

2. Anand Sarup, "Community Development in India" (Nagoya, Japan: United Nations Centre for Regional Development, 1981), cites the lack of evaluation as one of the "distortive factors" plaguing the campaign for structural socioeconomic change. This criticism, in our experience, applies to many development programs today.

3. Lloyd Rodwin, "Urban Growth Strategies Reconsidered," in *Growth Centers in Regional Economic Development,* ed. Niles M. Hansen (New York: Free Press, 1972), p. 16.

4. R. Weitz, D. Pelley, and L. Applebaum, "Employment and Income Generation in New Settlement Projects," World Employment Programme Research Working Paper (Geneva: International Labor Organization, 1978). A shorter version is "Model for the Planning of New Settlement Projects," *World Development* 8 (1980), pp. 105-23.

5. Wu Chung-Tong and David F. Ip, "Case Study from China" (Nagoya, Japan: United Nations Centre for Regional Development, 1981).

6. R. P. Misra, "Growth Poles and Growth Centres in the Context of India's Urban and Regional Development Problems," in *Growth Poles and Growth Centres in Regional Planning,* ed. Antoni Kuklinski (The Hague: Mouton & Co., 1972), p. 149. This description of India applies to a majority of developing countries.

7. Chung-Tong and Ip, "Case Study from China," p. 82.

8. Elsewhere in the developing world, the intersectoral approach has begun to enter the development process early in the planning phase. For instance, an Israeli-led team of planners working in the Nykuru-Nyandarua region of Kenya conceived a development based on a fully integrated intersectoral approach to economic growth. Gradually, this approach is being instituted in other countries as well. David Pelley et al., *Planning Process: Nykuru-Nyandarua Region—Kenya* (Rehovot, Israel: Settlement Study Centre, 1982), pp. 170-78.

9. T. R. Lakashmanan, "A Systems Model of Rural Development" (Nagoya, Japan: United Nations Centre for Regional Planning, 1981).

10. Ibid.

11. Chung-Tong and Ip, "Case Study from China."

12. See Colin MacAndrews, Atar Sibero, and H. Benjamin Fisher, "Regional Development, Planning and Implementation in Indonesia: The Evolution of a National Policy" (Nagoya, Japan: United Nations Centre for Regional Development, 1981).

13. See Sarup, "Community Development in India."

14. [It] . . . is important to take a functional approach in regionalization. One such approach for the delimitation of a region/planning area which seems appropriate for a country like Tanzania could be that a region should comprise "next to a full hierarchy" of the services which exist in the nation as a whole. This means that within each of the planning sectors there should be all services except for the most specialized. For instance, in the case of health facilities, there should be dispensaries, health centers and hospitals but not necessarily specialized hospitals. . . .

Jan Lundqvist, "Regional Information and Regional Planning in Tanzania," in *Regional Information and Regional Planning,* ed. Antoni Kuklinski (The Hague: Mouton & Co., 1974), p. 54.

15. For example, Israel Prion, *Development Trends of Spatial Rural Cooperation in Israel* (Rehovot, Israel: Settlement Study Centre, 1968).

16. See Akin L. Mabogunje, "Urbanization Problems in Africa" (Paper prepared for the Sixth Rehovot Conference on Urbanization and Development in Developing Countries, 1971, Rehovot, Israel), published in *Conference Papers* (Rehovot, Israel: Settlement Study Centrer 1971).

17. Moshe Prives, *Bas Boen, A Project of International Cooperation in*

Agricultural Development in a Hard-Core Poverty Area, Valley of Cul-de-Sac, Haiti (Rehovot, Israel: Centre for International Agricultural Cooperation, Ministry of Agriculture, 1978), pp. 6-8.

18. Moshe Prives, "A Project in Zambia: Integrated Area Settlement in the Copperbelt" (Rehovot, Israel: Centre for International Agricultural Cooperation, Ministry of Agriculture, 1974).

19. The *moshav ovdim* is a cooperative settlement of family farms. The farmers are organized in a multipurpose cooperative, supplying services and operating a number of joint activities, although each farm family owns its own home, tills its own soil, and makes its own decisions. The cooperative is managed by a village committee elected by the farmers.

20. Angel Rodriguez et al., *Proyecto Asentamiento Campesino "El Sisal" (Azua)* (Santo Domingo, Dominican Republic: Institute Agrario Dominicano, 1969).

21. *The Lachish Region—Background Study for Research in Regional Development Planning* (Rehovot, Israel: Settlement Study Centre, 1970); A. Rokach, ed., *Lachish, From Planning to Implementation* (Rehovot, Israel: Settlement Study Centre, 1978).

22. W. Christaller, *Central Places in Southern Germany* (Englewood Cliffs, N.J.: Prentice-Hall, 1966).

23. A. C. Jenkins, *The Golden Bank: The Polder Farm* (London: Methuen, 1966), pp. 97-104.

24. Cf. *Main Report, Kabankalan Settlement Project, Feasibility Study* (Manila: Ministry of Agrarian Reform, 1981).

25. Cf. *Settlement Project—La Joya, Peru, Activity Report for the Period June 1976-June 1977* (Rehovot, Israel: Center for International Agricultural Cooperation, Ministry of Agriculture, 1977).

CHAPTER 5

1. World Bank, *World Bank Tables* (Baltimore, Md.: Johns Hopkins University Press, 1976).

2. United Nations, Department of International Economic and Social Affairs, *Yearbook of National Accounts Statistics 1977* (New York: United Nations, 1978).

3. Gal-Oya Development Board, *Annual Reports,* 1949-50, 1955-56, 1959-60, 1962-63, 1964-65 (Colombo, Sri Lanka); *Ude Walawe Project, Ceylon—A Comparative Study of Two Regional Planning Alternatives* (Rehovot, Israel: Settlement Study Centre, 1971), project leader, Raanan Weitz.

4. United Nations Industrial Development Organization, *Summaries of the Industrial Development Plans of Thirty Countries* (New York: United Nations, 1970).

5. *Whitaker's Almanac,* Section on National Health Services (London: 1976).

6. R. F. Mikesell and J. E. Zisner, "The Nature of the Savings Function in Developing Countries: A Survey of Theoretical and Empirical Literature," *Journal of Economics* 11, 1 (March 1973).

7. M. Morishima, Y. Murata, and J. Nosse, *Working of Econometric Models* (Cambridge: Cambridge University Press, 1972).

8. K. Okawa and H. Rosovsky, *Japanese Economic Growth Trend Acceleration in the Twentieth Century* (Stanford, Calif.: Stanford University Press, 1973).

CHAPTER 6

1. Anand Sarup, "Community Development in India" (Nagoya, Japan: United Nations Centre for Regional Development, 1981).

2. J. Djodevic, "Remarks on the Yugoslav Model of Federalism," *Publius* 5 (Spring 1975), pp. 77-88.

3. *Statistical yearbook of the Socialist Federal Republic of Yugoslavia* (Belgrade: Federal Statistical Office, Socialist Federal Republic of Yugoslavia, 1978), pp. 98-105.

4. Cf. Wu Chung-Tong and David F. Ip, "Rural Development and Regional Autonomy in China: Recent Directions in Guangdong and Shandong" (Nagoya, Japan: United Nations Centre for Regional Development, 1981).

5. See Emeterio Barcelon and Aurora R. Pelayo, "Approaches to Local Level Development in the Philippines: A case study of Southern Mindanao," in R. P. Misra, ed., *Rural Development: National Policies and Experiences* (Nagoya, Japan: United Nations Centre for Regional Development, 1981.)

6. See Gabriele Pescatore and Raanan Weitz, *Report on a Mission to the Northeast of Brazil* (Rehovot, Israel: Settlement Study Centre, 1966), p. 6.

7. Albert Waterson, *Development Planning: Lessons of Experience* (Baltimore, Md.: Johns Hopkins University Press, 1965), pp. 289-90.

8. L.B.M. Mennes, Jan Tinbergen, and J. George Waardenburg, *The Element of Space in Development Planning* (Amsterdam: North-Holland Publishing Company, 1969), p. 50.

9. For an excellent description of the Chinese institutional structures, see Wu Chung-Tong and David F. Ip, "Case Study from China" (Nagoya, Japan: United Nations Centre for Regional Development, 1981).

10. Ibid.

11. Jack Gray, "Rural Enterprise in China, 1977-1979," in Jack Gray

and Gordon White, eds., *China's New Development Strategy* (London: Academic Press, 1982), p. 229.

12. Much of the material for this section is taken from Raanan Weitz, "Integration of Physical and Economic Planning" (Rehovot, Israel: Settlement Study Centre, 1973), which is an adaptation of a paper prepared for the United Nations Centre for Housing, Building and Planning Experts meeting on the integration of economic and physical planning, New York, September 1973.

13. See Pescatore and Weitz, *Report on a Mission to the Northeast of Brazil.*

14. Cf. Extacion Experimental Agropecuaria, *Planificacion para el desarrollo Integral de Areas Restringidas* (Buenos Aires: Instituto Nacional de Technologia Agropecuria, Republic of Argentina, 1966).

15. Gal-Oya, Sri Lanka.

16. Colin MacAndrews, Atar Sibero, and H. Benjamin Fisher, "Regional Development, Planning and Implementation in Indonesia: The Evolution of a National Policy" (Nagoya, Japan: United Nations Centre for Regional Development, 1981).

17. Ibid.

18. Ibid.

19. See Joseph S. Zalmanov, *CIAC Report, Dominican Republic—El Sisal Development Project* (Rehovot, Israel: Centre for International Agricultural Cooperation, Ministry of Agriculture, 1973).

20. T. R. Lakashmanan, "A Systems Model of Rural Development" (Nagoya, Japan: United Nations Centre for Regional Development, 1981).

21. Zalmanov, *CIAC Report, Dominican Republic.*

22. Moshe Z. Prives, *Bas Boen: A Project of International Cooperation in Agricultural Development in a Hard-Core Poverty Area, Valley of Cul-de-Sac, Haiti* (Rehovot, Israel: Centre for International Agricultural Cooperation, Ministry of Agriculture, 1978).

23. Moshe Z. Prives, "A Project in Zambia: Integrated Area Settlement in the Copperbelt" (Rehovot, Israel: Centre for International Agricultural Cooperation, Ministry of Agriculture, 1974).

CHAPTER 7

1. Thomas Fillol, *Social Factors in Economic Development, The Argentine Case* (Cambridge, Mass.: MIT Press, 1961).

2. A. W. Johnson, "Security and Risk-Taking among Poor Peasants," in *Studies in Economic Anthropology,* ed. G. Dalton (Washington, D.C.: American Anthropological Association, 1971), pp. 143-49. A. W. Johnson, *Sharecroppers of the Seratao Economics and Dependence on a Brazilian Plantation* (Stanford, Calif.: Stanford University Press, 1971). S.

Forman, *The Brazilian Peasantry* (New York: Columbia University Press, 1975). P.C.J. Saenz and C. F. Knight, *Tenure Security, Land Tilling and Agricultural Development in Costa Rica* (Ciudad Universitaria "Rodrigo Facio": University of Costa Rica, School of Law, 1971). M. A. Seligson, "Prestige among Peasants: A Multidimensional Analysis of Preference Data," *American Journal of Sociology* 83 (November 1977), pp. 632-52. C. R. Wharton, "Risk, Uncertainty and the Subsistence Farmer: Technological Innovation and Resistance to Change in the Context of Survival," in *Studies in Economic Anthropology*, ed. G. Dalton (Washington, D.C.: American Anthropological Association, 1971), pp. 151-78.

3. Raanan Weitz, "Rural Development: The Lesson of the Asian Countries," paper presented to the United Nations Seminar or Rural Development, Nagoya, Japan. The paper can be obtained from the Settlement Study Centre, Rehovot, Israel.

4. Moshe Z. Prives, *Bas Boen, A Project of International Cooperation in Agricultural Development in a Hard-Core Poverty Area, Valley Cul-de-Sac, Haiti* (Rehovot, Israel: Centre for International Agricultural Cooperation, Ministry of Agriculture, 1978).

5. See Raanan Weitz, "Social Planning in Rural Regional Development: The Israeli Experience," *Regional Socio-Economic Development—International Social Development Review* 4, United Nations, 1972, pp. 57-72.

6. Wu Chung-Tong and David F. Ip, "Case Study from China" (Nagoya, Japan: United Nations Centre for Regional Development, 1981).

7. Anand Sarup, "Community Development in India" (Nagoya, Japan: United Nations Centre for Regional Development, 1981). Sarup's description of the program's underlying principles, which were formulated by Mahatma Ghandi and the India National Congress, can be found in the appendix.

8. Chung-Tong and Ip, "Case Study from China," p. 19.

9. J. M. Cohen and N. T. Uphoff, "Participation's Place in Rural Development: Seeking Clarity through Specificity," *World Development* 8 (1980), pp. 213-35.

10. D. Hapgood, ed., *The Role of Popular Participation in Development,* Report of a Conference on the Implementation of Title IX of the Foreign Assistance Act (Cambridge, Mass.: MIT Press, 1969).

11. Cohen and Uphoff, "Participation's Place in Rural Development."

12. Chung-Tong and Ip, "Case Study from China," p. 21.

13. Ibid., p. 33.

14. Ibid., p. 139.

15. Raanan Weitz, *From Peasant to Farmer* (New York: Columbia University Press, 1971).

16. Joseph S. Zalmanov, "Dominican Republic: El-Sisal Development Project" (Rehovot, Israel: Centre for International Agricultural Cooperation, Ministry of Agriculture, 1973).

17. See Moshe Z. Prives, "A Project in Zambia: Integrated Area Settlement in the Copperbelt" (Rehovot, Israel: Centre for International Agricultural Cooperation, Ministry of Agriculture, 1974).

18. Moshe Z. Prives, *Bas Boen, A Project of International Cooperation in Agricultural Development in a Hard-Core Poverty Area, Valley of Cul-de-Sac, Haiti* (Rehovot, Israel: Centre for International Agricultural Cooperation, Ministry of Agriculture, 1978), pp. 12-13.

19. Prives, "Project in Zambia."

20. Ibid.

21. Prives, *Bas Boen*, pp. 73-74.

22. Ibid., p. 32.

CHAPTER 8

1. See *Crete Development Plan, 1965-1975,* 1, *Summary* (Tel Aviv: Agricultural Development Company [International], 1965).

2. R. Carillo-Arronte and V. Grosman, "Regional Information and Regional Planning in Mexico," in *Regional Information and Regional Planning,* ed. Antoni Kuklinski (The Hauge: Mouton and Company, 1974), p. 42.

3. Solon Barraclough, "Farmers' Organizations in Planning and Implementing Rural Development," in *Rural Development in a Changing World,* ed. Raanan Weitz (Cambridge, Mass.: MIT Press, 1971), pp. 386-87.

4. Albert Waterson, *Development Planning: Lessons of Experience* (Baltimore, Md.: Johns Hopkins University Press, 1969), pp. 51-52.

5. R. P. Dore, *Land Reform in Japan* (London: Oxford University Press, 1959), p. xi.

6. Saburo Okita, "Development Strategy: A Japanese Perspective," in *Nation-Building and Regional Development: The Japanese Experience,* ed., H. Nagamine (Nagoya, Japan: Maruzen Asia for and on behalf of the United Nations Centre for Regional Development, 1981), pp. 4-5, 12.

7. Wu Chung-Tong and David F. Ip, *Rural Development and Regional Autonomy in China* (Nagoya, Japan: United Nations Centre for Regional Development, 1981), p. 260.

8. Walter Stohr and D. R. Fraser Taylor, "Development from Above or Below? The Dialectics of Regional Planning in Developing Countries," in *Regional Development Alternatives: International Perspectives,* ed. A. L. Mabogunje and R. P. Misra (Nagoya, Japan: Maruzen Asia for and on behalf of the United Nations Centre for Regional Development, 1981), p. 10.

BIBLIOGRAPHY

Adelman, I., and C. Morris. *Society, Politics, and Economic Development—Quantitative Approach.* Baltimore, Md.: Johns Hopkins University Press, 1975.

Alonso, William. "Planning and the Spatial Organization of the Metropolis in the Developing Countries." *Conference Papers.* Sixth Rehovot Conference. Rehovot, Israel: Settlement Study Centre, 1971.

Atkinson, A. B. "On the Measurement of Inequality." *Journal of Economic Theory* 2, 2 (1970).

Ayal, E. B. "Value Systems and Economic Development in Japan and Thailand." *Journal of Social Issues* 19, 1 (January 1963).

Barcelon, Emeterio, and Aurora R. Pelayo. "Case Study from Philippines." Nagoya, Japan: United Nations Centre for Regional Development, 1956.

Barraclough, Solon. "Farmers' Organizations in Planning and Implementing Rural Development." In *Rural Development in a Changing World*, edited by Raanan Weitz. Cambridge, Mass.: MIT Press, 1971.

Brandt, W. *North-South: A Program for Survival.* London: Pan Books, 1980.

Brutzkus, E. "Centralized versus Decentralized Patterns of Urbanization in Developing Countries: An Attempt to Elucidate a Guideline Principle." *Economic Development and Cultural Change* 23, 4 (July 1975).

Carrillo-Arronte, R., and V. Grossman. "Regional Information and Regional Planning in Mexico." In *Regional Information and Regional Planning,* edited by Antoni Kuklinski. The Hague: Mouton & Company, 1974.

Chenery, H. B., and M. Syrquin. *Patterns of Development, 1950-1970.* London: Oxford University Press, 1975.

Christaller, W. *Central Places in Southern Germany.* Englewood Cliffs, N. J.: Prentice-Hall, 1966.

Chung-Tong, Wu, and David F. Ip. *Rural Development and Regional Autonomy in China: Recent Directions in Guangdong and Shandong.* Nagoya, Japan: United Nations Centre for Regional Development, 1981.

_____. "Case Study from China." Nagoya, Japan: United Nations Centre for Regional Development, 1981.

Clinard, Marshall. "The Absorption Problems of In-Migration." *Conference Papers.* Sixth Rehovot Conference. Rehovot, Israel: Settlement Study Centre, 1971.

Clout, H. "Rural-Urban Migration in Western Europe." In *Geographical Essay,* edited by J. Salt and H. Clout. London: Oxford University Press, 1976.

Cohen, J. M., and N. T. Uphoff. "Participation's Place in Rural Development: Seeking Clarity through Specificity." *World Development* 8 (1980).

Connell, J., et al. *Migration from Rural Areas.* Delhi: Oxford University Press, 1976.

Crete Development Plan, 1965-1975, vol. 1—*Summary.* Tel Aviv: Agricultural Development Company [International], 1965.

Crooks, Robert J. "Urbanization and Social Change: Transitional Urban Settlements in Developing Countries." *Conference Papers.* Sixth Rehovot Conference. Rehovot, Israel: Settlement Study Centre, 1971.

Dalton, G. *Economic Systems and Society.* Harmondsworth, United Kingdom: Penguin Books, 1974.

Davis, Kingsley. "The Role of Urbanization in the Development Process." *Conference Papers.* Sixth Rehovot Conference, Rehovot, Israel: Settlement Study Centre, 1971.

Djodevic, J. "Remarks on the Yugoslav Model of Federalism." *Publius* 5 (Spring 1975).

Dore, R. P. *Land Reform in Japan.* London: Oxford University Press, 1959.

Dovring, F. "The Share of Agriculture in a Growing Population." *FAO Monthly Bulletin of Agricultural Economics and Statistics* I-II (August-September 1950).

The Element of Space in Development Planning. Amsterdam: North-Holland, 1969.

Estacion Experimental Agropecuaria. *Planificacion para el Desarollo Integral de Areas Restringidas.* Buenos Aires: Instituto Nacional de Technologia Agropecuaria, 1966.

Fillol, Thomas. *Social Factors in Economic Development, The Argentine Case.* Cambridge, Mass.: MIT Press, 1961.

Flores, Edmundo. "Economic Growth and Urbanization." *Conference Papers.* Sixth Rehovot Conference. Rehovot, Israel: Settlement Study Centre, 1971.

Forman, S. *The Brazilian Peasantry.* New York: Columbia University Press, 1975.

Freeman, Daniel. "The Transfer of Investment Capital from Developed to Developing Countries." *The Economic Quarterly* 112 (February 1982).

Friedman, M. *Essays in Positive Economics.* Chicago: University of Chicago Press, 1966.

Gal Oya Development Board. *Annual Reports,* 1949-50, 1955-56, 1959-60, 1962-63, 1964-65. Colombo, Sri Lanka.

Gray, Jack. "Rural Enterprise in China, 1977-1979." In *China's New Development Strategy, edited by Jack Gray and Gordon White. London: Academic Press, 1982.*

Hapgood, D., ed. The Role of Popular Participation in Development. Report of a Conference on the Implementation of Title IX of the Foreign Assistance Act. Cambridge, Mass.: MIT Press, 1969.

Heilbroner, Robert. *The Great Ascent.* New York: Harper & Row, 1963.

Henderson, P. D. "Economics Askew." *Encounter* (December 1980).

Herford, R. T., trans. *Pirke Abot: The Ethics of the Talmud, Sayings of the Fathers.* New York: Schocken Books, 1962.

Hermansen, Tormod. "Development Poles and Development." In *Growth Poles and Growth Centres in Regional Planning,* edited by Antoni Kuklinski. The Hague: Mouton & Co., 1972.

Herrera, Felipe. "Nationalism and Urbanization in Latin America." *Conference Papers.* Sixth Rehovot Conference. Rehovot, Israel: Settlement Study Centre, 1971.

Hicks, N., and P. Streeten. "Indicators of Developement: The Search for Basic Needs Yardstick." *World Development* 7 (1979).

Hyman, H. H. *Inducing Social Change in Developing Communities.* Geneva: UNRISD, 1966.

Jacobs, N. *Modernization with Development: Thailand as an Asian Case Study.* New York: Praeger, 1971.

Jenkins, A. C. *The Golden Bank: The Polder Farm.* London: Methuen, 1966.

Johnson, A. W. "Security and Risk-Taking among Poor Peasants." In *Studies in Economic Anthropology*, edited by G. Dalton. Washington, D.C.: American Anthropological Association, 1971.

Sharecroppers of the Seratao Economics and Dependence on a Brazilian Plantation. Stanford, Calif.: Stanford University Press, 1971.

Kahl, J. *The Measurement of Modernism*. Austin: University of Texas Press, 1969.

Kohler, W. W. *The Place of Value in a World of Facts*. New York: Liveright, 1938.

Kolm, S. Ch. "Unequal Inequalities." *Journal of Economic Theory* 12, 3 (1976).

Kuklinski, Antoni, and R. Petrella, eds. *Growth Poles and Regional Policies: A Seminar*. The Hague: Mouton & Co., 1972.

Kuznets, S. M. *Economic Growth of Nations: Total Output and Production Structure*. Cambridge, Mass.: Belknap Press, 1971.

The Lachish Region—Background Study for Research in Regional Development Planning. Rehovot, Israel: Settlement Study Centre, 1970.

Lakashmanan, T. R. "A Systems Model of Rural Development." Nagoya, Japan: United Nations Centre for Regional Planning, 1981.

Leontief, W. W. "The Distribution of Work and Income." *Scientific American* 247, 3 (September 1982).

Lichtfield, Nathaniel. "Economic Growth and Urbanization." *Conference Papers*. Sixth Rehovot Conference. Rehovot, Israel: Settlement Study Centre, 1971.

Lundqvist, Jan. "Regional Information and Regional Planning in Tanzania." In *Regional Information and Regional Planning*, edited by Antoni Kuklinski. The Hague: Mouton & Co., 1974.

Mabogunje, Akin L. "Urbanization Problems in Africa." *Conference Papers*. Sixth Rehovot Conference. Rehovot, Israel: Settlement Study Centre, 1971.

MacAndrews, Colin, Atar Sibero, and H. Benjamin Fisher. "Regional Development, Planning and Implementation in Indonesia: The Evolution of a National Policy." Nagoya, Japan: United Nations Centre for Regional Development, 1981.

Marshall, A. *Principles of Economics*. London: Macmillan, 1920.

Mason, E. S., and R. E. Asher. *The World Bank Since Bretton Woods*. Washington, D.C.: Brookings Institution, 1973.

McGee, T. G. *The Urbanization Process in the Third World*. London: G. Bell, 1971.

Mennes, L. B. M., Jan Tinbergen, and J. George Waardenberg. *The Element of Space in Development Planning*. Amsterdam: North-Holland, 1969.

Mikesell, R. F., and J. E. Zisner. "The Nature of the Savings Function in Developing Countries: A Survey of Theoretical and Empirical Literature." *Journal of Economics* 11, 1 (March 1973).

Minogue, K. "Between Rhetoric and Fantasy." *Encounter* (December 1980).

Misra, R. P. "Growth Poles and Growth Centres in the Context of India's Urban and Regional Development Problems." In *Growth Poles and Growth Centres in Regional Planning*, edited by Antoni Kuklinski. The Hague: Mouton & Co., 1972.

Morishima, M., Y. Murata, and J. Nosse. *Working of Econometric Models*. Cambridge: Cambridge University Press, 1972.

Morris, M. D. "A Physical Quality of Life Index (POLI)." *The United States and World Development, Agenda, 1976*. New York: Praeger, 1976.

Myrdal, Gunnar. *Asian Drama: An Inquiry into the Poverty of Nations*. New York: Pantheon, 1968.

Okawa, K., and H. Rosovsky. *Japanese Economic Growth Trend Acceleration in the Twentieth Century*. Stanford, Calif.: Stanford University Press, 1973.

Okita, Saburo. "Development Strategy: A Japanese Perspective." In *Nation-Building and Regional Development: The Japanese Experience,* edited by H. Nagamine. Nagoya, Japan: Maruzen Asia, 1981.

Pearson, L. *Partners in Development, Report of the Commission on International Development*. New York: Praeger, 1968.

Pelley, David, et al. *Planning Process: Nykuru-Nyandarua Region—Kenya.* Rehovot, Israel: Settlement Study Centre, 1982.

Pescatore, Gabriele, and Raanan Weitz. *Report on a Mission to the Northeast of Brazil*. Rehovot, Israel: Settlement Study Centre, 1966.

Prion, Israel. *Development Trends of Spatial Rural Cooperation in Israel*. Rehovot, Israel: Settlement Study Centre, 1968.

Prives, Moshe Z. *Bas Boen, A Project of International Cooperation in Agricultural Development in a Hard-Core Poverty Area, Valley of Cul-de-Sac, Haiti*. Rehovot, Israel: Centre for International Agricultural Cooperation, Ministry of Agriculture, 1978.

————. "A Project in Zambia: Integrated Area Settlement in the Copperbelt." Mimeograph. Rehovot, Israel: Centre for International Agricultural Cooperation, Ministry of Agriculture, 1974.

Rodriguez, Angel T., et al. *Proyecto de Asentamiento Campesino "El Sisal" (Azua)*. Santo Domingo: Instituto Agrario Dominicano, 1969.

Rodwin, Lloyd. "Urban Growth Strategies Reconsidered." In *Growth Centers in Regional Economic Development*, edited by Niles M. Hansen. New York: Free Press, 1972.

244   Bibliography

Rogers, E. M. *Modernization Among Peasants—The Impact of Communication.* New York: Holt, Rinehart and Winston, 1969.

Rokach, A., ed. *Lakhish, From Planning to Implementation.* Rehovot, Israel: Settlement Study Centre, 1978.

Sadove, Robert. "A Response to the Urban Needs of Developing Countries." *Conference Papers.* Sixth Rehovot Conference. Rehovot, Israel: Settlement Study Centre, 1971.

Saenz, P. C. J., and C. F. Knight. *Tenure Security, Land Tilling and Agricultural Development in Costa Rica.* Ciudad Universitaria "Rodrigo Facio": University of Costa Rica, School of Law, 1971.

Sarup, Anand. "Community Development in India." Nagoya, Japan: United Nations Centre for Regional Development, 1981.

Schultz, T. *Transforming Traditional Agriculture.* New Haven, Connecticut: Yale University Press, 1964.

Seligson, M. A. "Prestige among Peasants: A Multidimensional Analysis of Preference Data." *American Journal of Sociology* 83 (November 1977).

Settlement Project—La Joya, Peru, Activity Report for the Period June 1976-June 1977. Rehovot, Israel: Centre for International Agricultural Cooperation, Ministry of Agriculture, 1977.

Smith, Adam. *The Wealth of Nations.* New York: Random House, 1937.

Stohr, Walter, and D. R. Fraser Taylor. "Development from Above or Below? The Dialectics of Regional Planning in Developing Countries." In *Regional Development Alternatives: International Perspectives,* edited by A. L. Mabogunje and R. P. Misra. Nagoya, Japan: Maruzen Asia, 1981.

Stretton, H. *Urban Planning in Rich and Poor Countries.* Oxford: Oxford University Press, 1978.

Tanne, David. "Policies of Rapid Urbanization in Israel." *Conference Papers.* Sixth Rehovot Conference. Rehovot, Israel: Settlement Study Centre, 1971.

Thomas, Morgan D. "Growth Pole Theory: An Examination of Some of Its Basic Concepts." In *Growth Center and Regional Economic Development,* edited by Morgan D. Thomas and Miles Hansen. New York: Free Press, 1972.

Todaro, M. P. *Economic Development in the Third World.* London: Longman, 1977.

Toffler, Alvin. *The Third Wave.* New York: Bantam Books, 1980.

Uda Walawe Project, Ceylon—A Comparative Study of Two Regional Planning Alternatives. Rehovot, Israel: Settlement Study Centre, 1971.

United Nations Department of International Economic and Social Affairs. *Yearbook of National Accounts Statistics 1977.* New York: United Nations, 1978.

United Nations Industrial Development Organization. *Summaries of the Industrial Development Plans of Thirty Countries.* New York: United Nations, 1970.

United Nations Department of Public Information. *Basic Facts about the United Nations, Summary of Its Purposes, Structures and Activities.* New York: United Nations, 1976.

UNRISD. *Contents and Measurements of Socioeconomic Development.* New York: Praeger, 1972.

Waterson, Albert. *Development Planning: Lessons of Experience.* Baltimore, Md.: John Hopkins University Press, 1963.

Weitz, Raanan. "Family Farms Versus Large-Scale Farms in Rural Development." *Artha Vijnana,* 5, 3 (September 1963).

_____. "Regional Planning—Report on a Visit to Turkey." Paper prepared for the Organisation for Economic Cooperation and Development in cooperation with the State of Israel, Ministry for Foreign Affairs, Jerusalem, 1964.

_____. "Sur le Principe du Development Rural Integre." *Economie Rurale* (Juillet-Septembre 1964).

_____. "Rural Development through Regional Planning in Israel." *Journal of Farm Economics,* August 1965.

_____. "Regional Development Programming." Washington, D.C.: Pan American Union, Studies and Monographs, 1966.

_____. "Technical Aid to Developing Countries: Evaluation and Reorientation." Paper presented to the Eighth World Conference of the Society of International Development, New York, 1966.

_____. "The Transformation of Ceylonese Peasant Agriculture." Report submitted for the Organization for Economic Cooperation and Development, Seminar on Development Strategy and Administration, Colombo, Ceylon, 1966. Available from the Settlement Study Centre, Rehovot, Israel.

_____. "Problems of Rural Development." *Problems of Development.* Paris: OECD, 1967.

_____, with Avshalom Rokach. *Agricultural Development: Planning and Implementation.* Dordrecht, Holland: Reidel, 1968.

_____. "Development and Values: Regional Planning in Israel." Paper presented to Israel Academic Committee on the Middle East from the proceedings on the seminar for visiting academics held at the Tel Aviv University, May 1971.

————. *From Peasant to Farmer: A Revolutionary Strategy for Development.* A Twentieth Century Fund Study. New York: Columbia University Press, 1971.

————, ed. *Rural Development in a Changing World.* Cambridge, Mass.: M.I.T. Press, 1971.

————. "Social Planning in Rural Regional Development: The Israeli Experience." *International Social Development Review,* 4 (United Nations, 1972).

————, ed. *Urbanization and the Developing Countries: Report on the Sixth Rehovot Conference.* New York: Praeger, 1973.

————. "Integration of Physical and Economic Planning." Paper presented to the United Nations Centre for Housing, Building and Planning Experts Meeting on the Integration of Economic and Physical Planning. New York, September 1973.

————. *Integrated Rural Development: Rehovot Approach.* Rehovot, Israel: Settlement Study Centre, 1979.

————. "Economic Growth Values and Physical Planning." Paper published under the auspices of the Norman Hanson Visiting Fellow Award Lecture Series, 1982.

————. "Man-Machine for Rural Regional Development Planning." *Integrated Rural Regional Development for Areas of New Settlements.* Rehovot, Israel: Settlement Study Centre, 1984.

Weitz, Raanan, and Levia Applebaum. "Planning for Full Employment in Rural Areas." Paper prepared for a Ford Foundation seminar on Rural Development and Employment, Ibadan, Nigeria, April 9-12, 1973. A copy of this paper can be obtained from the Settlement Study Area, Rehovot, Israel.

Weitz, Raanan, D. Pelley, and L. Applebaum. "Employment and Income Generation in New Settlement Projects." World Employment Programme Research Working Paper. Geneva: International Labor Organization, 1978.

Weitz, Raanan, David Pelley, and Levia Applebaum. "A Model for the Planning of New Settlement Projects." *World Development* 8, 9 (September 1980).

Weitz, Raanan, et al. "A Comparative Study of Five Development Projects." Rehovot, Israel: Settlement Study Centre, 1980.

Wharton, C. R. "Risk, Uncertainty and the Subsistence Farmer: Technological Innovation and Resistance to Change in the Context of Survival." In *Studies in Economic Anthropology,* edited by G. Dalton. Washington, D.C.: American Anthropological Association, 1971.

Whitaker's Almanac, Section on National Health Services. London: 1976.

Wingo, Lowdon. "National Development Objectives and Metropolitan Concentration." *Conference Papers*. Sixth Rehovot Conference. Rehovot, Israel: Settlement Study Centre, 1971.

Winnie, J., and W. W. William. *Latin American Development*. Los Angeles, California: University of California Press, 1967.

World Bank. *Questions and Answers*. Washington, D.C.: World Bank, 1976.

_____. *World Bank Tables*. Baltimore, Md.: Johns Hopkins University Press, 1976.

_____. *World Development Report, 1980*. Washington, D.C.: World Bank, 1980.

Yugoslavian *1978 Statistical Handbook*.

Zalmanov, Joseph S. *Dominican Republic: El Sisal Development Project*. Rehovot, Israel: Centre for International Agricultural Cooperation, Ministry of Agriculture, 1973.

INDEX

About the Author

RAANAN WEITZ is Head of the Settlement Study Centre in Rehovot, Israel. He has long been committed to realizing the Centre's primary goal of developing a man-machine computerized system for regional planning. Among his numerous earlier works are *Integrated Rural Development: Rehovot Approach, Development and Urbanization in the Developing Countries,* and *From Peasant to Farmer: A Revolutionary Strategy for Development.*